THE OJIBWAS

BIBLIOGRAPHICAL SERIES

The Newberry Library Center for the History of the American Indian

The Center is Supported by Grants from

The National Endowment for the Humanities

The Ford Foundation

The W. Clement and Jessie V. Stone Foundation

The Woods Charitable Fund, Inc.

The Ojibwas

A Critical Bibliography

HELEN HORNBECK TANNER

Published for the Newberry Library

Indiana University Press

BLOOMINGTON AND LONDON

Published in Canada by Fitzhenry & Whiteside Limited, Don Mills Ontario

Manufactured in the United States of America

Library of Congress Cataloging in Publication Data
Tanner, Helen Hornbeck.
The Ojibwas: a critical bibliography.
(The Newberry Library Center for the History of the American Indian bibliographical series)
1. Chippewa Indians—Bibliography. I. Title.
II. Series.
Z1210.C5T36 1976 [E99.C6] 016.97'0004'97
76-12376
ISBN 0-253-34165-5 1 2 3 4 5 80 79 78 77 76

The Editors to the Reader

A massive literature exists for the history and culture of American Indians, but the quality of that literature is very uneven. At its best it compares well with the finest scholarship and most interesting reading to be found anywhere. At its worst it may take the form of malicious fabrication. Sometimes, well-intentioned writers give false impressions of reality either because of their own limitations of mind or because they lack adequate information. The consequence is a kind of chaos through which advanced scholars as well as new students must warily pick their way. It is, after all, a history of hundreds, if not thousands, of human communities spread over an entire continent and enduring through millenia of pre-Columbian years as well as the five centuries that Europeans have documented since 1492. That is not a small amount of history.

Often, however, historians have been so concerned with the affairs of European colonies or the United States that they have almost omitted Indians from their own history. "Frontier history" and the "history of Indian–White relations" frequently focus upon the intentions and desires of Euramericans, treating Native Americans as though they were merely natural parts of the landscape, like forests, or mountains, or wild animals — obstacles to "progress" or "civilization." One of the major purposes of the Newberry Library's Center for the History of the American Indian is to modify that narrow conception; to put Indians properly back into the central role in their own history and into the history of the United States of America as well — as participants in, rather than obstacles to, the creation of American society and culture.

The series of bibliographies, of which this book is one part, is intended as a guide to reliable sources and studies in particular fields of the general literature. Some of these are devoted to culture areas; others treat selected individual tribes; and a third group will speak to significant contemporary and historical issues.

Apart from introducing us to the interesting Ojibwa people themselves, Dr. Tanner's survey of the literature on this extensive tribe is especially valuable for sources relevant to certain much-argued issues in anthropology and history. One of these is the nature of a tribe — what are the criteria that distinguish a tribe from a band or a clan? How does a tribe preserve its identity after changing its name and migrating from the territory with which it has been identified? How does it establish a recognized claim to live and govern in a new territory? The problems with the nomenclature for the Ojibwas is rich in object lessons for the study of other tribes also, and it is surely a caution to the historian who must track the same people through source documents that identify them under so many different names.

This work is designed in a format, uniform throughout the entire series, to be useful to both beginning students and advanced scholars. It has two main parts: the essay (conveniently organized by subheadings) and an alphabetical list of all works cited. All citations in the essay are directly keyed, by means of bracketed numbers, to the more complete information in the list. In addition, the series incorporates several information-at-a-glance features. Preceding the list will be found two sets of recommended titles. One of these is a list of five items for the beginner; the second, a group of volumes that constitute a basic library collection in the field. Finally, asterisks within the alphabetical list denote works suitable for secondary school students. This apparatus has been built-in because the bibliographical essay, in a form familiar to scholars, will probably prove fairly hard going for beginners who may wish to put it aside until they have gained sufficient background from introductory materials. Such students should come back to the essay eventually, however, because it surveys a vast sweep of information about a great variety of persons, places, communities, and events.

There is variety also in the kinds of sources because these critical bibliographies support the study of ethnohistory. Unlike older, more narrow disciplines, ethnohistory embraces the entire culture of a people; it demands contributions from a wide range of source materials. Not the least of these in the history of American Indians are their own music, crafts, linguistics, and oral traditions. Whenever possible, the authors have included such sources as well as those associated with politics, economics, geography, and so on.

In the last analysis this work, like all other bibliographical devices, is a tool. Each author is an expert who knows the literature and advises what source is most helpful for which purpose, but students must use this help according to their individual purposes and capacities. Many ways suggest themselves. The decision is the reader's own.

Introduction

A bibliographic essay on the Ojibwa Indians initially presents a geographic challenge: this nation has a territorial range greater than that of any other Indian tribe in North America. The Ojibwa country in Canada and the United States encompasses an expanse of land from the eastern end of Lake Ontario westward to the vicinity of Lake Winnipeg in Manitoba and the Turtle Mountains of North Dakota.

Scholars from a variety of disciplines have demonstrated their interest in the Ojibwas. Archaeologists have delved into the earth for records of early camp sites and dwelling places. Interviews with venerable Ojibwa leaders have provided valuable response information for anthropologists. Native Americans rediscovering their own cultural roots have collected accounts of their traditions, while historians and cultural geographers continue to sift three centuries of documentary evidence in order to assemble the story of the Ojibwa people. As data from all these sources is synthesized, the picture of Ojibwa life — both past and present — becomes more complete.*

*Preparation of *The Ojibwas* has proceeded with the indispensable assistance of many people. Initial suggestions and recommendations came from Robert E. Bieder as Associate Director of the Center for the History of the American Indian, The Newberry Library; and from Nancy O. Lurie, Curator of Anthropology, Milwaukee Public Museum. Carolyn Bennett took charge of library research and assembling the basic bibliography from which the final selection was made. John D. Nichols shared drafts of linguistic bibliographies compiled as part of the Native American Studies Program at the University of Wisconsin, Milwaukee. Richard A. Rhodes of the Linguistics

Before presenting any titles, an explanation concerning the varied terminology of the tribal name seems in order. Neither "Ojibwa" nor "Chippewa" has any long history of common acceptance as the means of identifying kindred groups throughout their extensive territory. According to traditional accounts, the present day Ojibwas migrated westward over a period of two centuries, from a region east of Montreal to the environs of Lake Superior. Three generations, an estimated one hundred twenty years, elapsed before they were encountered by French explorers at the present Saint Mary's River, the outlet from Lake Superior to Lake Huron. The French called these Indians *Saulteurs,* referring to their location at the river rapids or falls (*sault* or *saut* in French), which provided the place name Sault de Sainte Marie after the establishment of a Jesuit mission in 1668. Even in twentieth-century literature, the names Saulteurs and Saulteaux are still used for the Ojibwa people north of Lake Superior in the Canadian provinces.

The term "Chippewa" is derived from the name of one of the local groups which moved from the north side

Department, The University of Michigan, provided an introduction to the Eastern Ojibwa language. Raymond D. Fogelson of the Department of Anthropology, The University of Chicago, contributed his appraisal of the extensive Hallowell literature on the Ojibwa people, too long to include in its entirety. I am particularly grateful for the continuing counsel of Richard I. Ford, Director of the Museum of Anthropology, The University of Michigan. Helen Tibbals handled the demands of bibliographic typing.

of Lake Superior to the Upper Peninsula of Michigan, probably in the seventeenth century. A more correct spelling is "Ojibwa," but the "Chippewa" form became standardized through use in the publcations of the Bureau of American Ethnology. Very recently, some publications have adopted the spellings "Ojibwe" and "Ochipwe," but "Ojibwa" is the most widely accepted form at the present. (In this essay, the form Ojibwa is used except where spelled otherwise by the author cited.) The term "Ojibwa" probably refers to the "puckered" construction of moccasin footwear. In Manitoba, the name "Bungi" (pronounced "bungee") is applied to the local Ojibwas; this is the Indian word for "a little," so often used in making requests of the early settlers.*

To compound the problem further, an additional term, "Missisauga," is commonly used alone and in conjunction with "Chippewa" in the region from Lake Huron southeast to Kingston, Ontario. Following the now familiar pattern, this term once had a more precise geographic association with the people in the vicinity of the Missisauga River on the north shore of Lake Huron. When the Iroquois were driven from the Ontario peninsula in the late seventeenth century, the Missisauga became the predominant group spreading throughout lower Ontario. The "Chippewa" of Saginaw Bay in eastern Michigan and the Saint Clair River region are pri-

*A Irving Hallowell, *Culture and Experience* [114], pg. 115; W. Vernon Kinietz, *Indian Tribes of the Western Great Lakes* [166], pp. 317–18.

marily of Missisauga origin.* From all this discussion of terminology, one significant point about expansion should be observed: the Ojibwas expanded eastward from a base point at Sault Sainte Marie in the late seventeenth and early eighteenth centuries, and westward in the eighteenth and continuing into the nineteenth centuries.

Any inquiry into the history and culture of the Ojibwa people begins naturally with the summaries of information provided in the two-volume *Handbook* edited by Hodge [134]. Until the long awaited revision appears, the entries "Chippewa" and "Missisauga" written by James Mooney and Cyrus Thomas [194] provide the most useful general introduction. The same entries appear in Hodge's *Handbook of the Indians of Canada* [135].

Another succinct source of information is provided by W. Vernon Kinietz, *Indians of the Western Great Lakes, 1615–1760* [166]. Kinietz's chapter on the Ojibwas is less adequate than his coverage of other Great Lakes tribes, but he did include references to pertinent selections from the *Jesuit Relations* [250] and other French writings that furnish keys to the earliest observations on regional Indian life. One misleading statement made by Kinietz, that the Ojibwas were incorporated into the Iroquois confederacy as the seventh tribe, demands fuller explica-

*Ernest J. Lajeunesse, ed., *The Windsor Border Region* [174], pg. 27; A. F. Chamberlain, "Notes on the History, Customs, and Beliefs of the Mississagua Indians" [59], pg. 150 and 154.

tion. Although the Missisauga made an alliance with the Iroquois in the eighteenth century, that relationship should not be considered a structural modification of the Six Nations confederacy, based in the Finger Lakes district of northern New York. However, the term "Seven Nations of Canada" does appear in late eighteenth-century documents.

The Accounts of Travelers and Explorers

The first French explorer and trader to acquire a thorough knowledge of the Ojibwas and their neighbors in the upper Great Lakes region was Nicholas Perrot; his "Memoir" has been translated and appears in the fine collection of primary documents edited by Emma Helen Blair, *The Indian Tribes of the Upper Mississippi Valley and Region of the Great Lakes* [209]. Among Perrot's many services to the French crown was his assignment to bring together Indian leaders of the upper Lakes for an impressive convocation at Sault Sainte Marie in 1671. The Blair publication provides additional information (probably attributable to Perrot) under the authorship of Bacqueville de la Potherie (Claude-Charles Le Roy de la Potherie), "History of the Savage People" [180]. Le Roy de la Potherie had a royal appointment in Canada in 1698.

The best known of the longer historical accounts is William W. Warren's "History of the Ojibways Based upon Tradition and Oral Statements" [263]. Warren's mother was an Ojibwa and his father a well-known trader in the Lake Superior region. Drawing upon traditional sources with the advantages of a formal education, Warren made a unique contribution to written tribal history. In the same volume of the *Collections of the Minnesota Historical Society* as Warren's history, may be found a companion work, "History of the Ojibways" by Edward D. Neill, based upon documentary sources [199].

The British fur traders' records are an important source of data on the Ojibwas and neighboring tribes. The earliest firsthand account of the Ojibwas and Ottawas of northwestern Michigan and the Upper Peninsula is Alexander Henry's *Travels and Adventures in Canada and the Indian Territories between the Years 1760 and 1776*, edited by Milo M. Quaife [120]. Henry's report of the destruction of the British garrison at Fort Michilimackinac in 1763 — when troops were caught off guard while watching an Indian lacrosse game — has become one of the classics of American historical literature. A nephew, usually identified as Alexander Henry "the Younger," has left an equally valuable record of the western frontier of Ojibwa territory in the early nineteenth century in the form of a journal kept at the trading post at Pembina from 1801 to 1808. This journal, along with the report of David Thompson, who visited the Ojibwas of Sandy Lake in 1799, has been published in the three volumes prepared by Elliott Coues, the reliable editor of so many accounts of explorations [74].

An authentic account of Ojibwa life in the western

region, and one of the great works of American Indian literature, is John Tanner's *A Narrative of the Captivity and Adventures of John Tanner* [248]. As a youth, Tanner was captured by Shawnees in Kentucky in 1789, then transferred to Saginaw Bay in Michigan, and later to Wisconsin. His descriptions of hunting expeditions into Manitoba and his travels southward through Minnesota to Chicago and north to Sault Sainte Marie have allowed scholars a rare insight into Indian life during the late eighteenth and early nineteenth centuries. Tanner's story was written at Sault Sainte Marie, Michigan by an army surgeon who required an interpreter because the former captive had become so thoroughly Indian in his ordinary speech.

British and American explorers have supplied additional basic information about the Ojibwas. The accounts of five expeditions to the upper Mississippi Valley between 1767 and 1832 offer a key sequence of observations, particularly useful in studying the status of the war-ridden Ojibwa – Sioux frontier. These are: Jonathan Carver, *Travels Through the Interior Parts of North America* [53]; Zebulon M. Pike, *The Expeditions of Zebulon Montgomery Pike to the Headwaters of the Mississippi River*, edited by Elliott Coues [210]; Henry R. Schoolcraft, *Narrative Journal of Travels Through the Northwestern Regions of the United States* [236]; William H. Keating, *Narrative of an Expedition to the Source of St. Peter's River* [161]; and Schoolcraft, *Narrative of an Expedition Through the Upper Mississippi to Itasca Lake* [237]. The best version of the latter trip is to be found among the collected reports edited by Philip P. Mason, *Expedition to Lake Itasca; The Discovery of the Source of the Mississippi* [189].

Henry R. Schoolcraft's journey to the lake he named "Itasca" climaxed twelve years of experience in the upper Great Lakes area. As a mineralogist, he had accompanied Michigan Territorial Governor Lewis Cass on his exploratory and treaty-making expedition from Detroit to Sault Sainte Marie, Fond du Lac, Sandy Lake, and finally to Chicago in 1820. Returning to Sault Sainte Marie as the first Indian agent in 1822, Schoolcraft began to collect materials and continued this practice throughout his many other assignments in the Indian Service; these have led to voluminous publications.* Since all women in the Ojibwa country at that time were of Indian ancestry, Schoolcraft married into an Irish-Ojibwa family, through which he acquired an extensive knowledge of tradition, language, and legend. Fortunately, there are two indices to the Schoolcraft material: Frances S. Nichols, *Index to Schoolcraft's "Indian Tribes of the United States"* [201] and the more specialized guide by Hallowell, "Concordance of Ojibwa Narratives in the Published Works of Henry R. Schoolcraft" [113].

*A complete bibliography of the works of Henry Rowe Schoolcraft — including books, pamphlets, periodical articles, and printed documents — may be found in Chase S. and Stella B. Osborn, *Schoolcraft, Longfellow, Hiawatha* [206].

Missionaries and Their Missions

Prominent in the list of authors cited in this bibliography are more than a dozen nineteenth- and early twentieth-century missionaries. Although they may show an understandable bias in their observations, they have nevertheless provided primary data for the whole of the Ojibwa territory. The best overview of this topic is Stephen R. Riggs, "Protestant Missions in the Northwest" [223].

The Protestant missionary effort among the Ojibwas began with the founding in 1824 of a Methodist mission at the River Credit (an aptly named trading center, west of Toronto); in 1827 its activities expanded to Grape Island in Lake Ontario's Bay of Quinte. The evangelistic movement spread from Canada to Michigan and across Minnesota in the 1830s. It was, however, an uneven and sometimes temporary development in Indian communities. Two pioneer missionaries of Ojibwa heritage active in this movement authored substantial volumes: George Copway, *The Traditional History and Characteristic Sketches of the Ojibway Nation* [73] and Peter Jones, *History of the Ojebway Indians* [155]. Another early account of Canadian missionary efforts is Frederick A. O'Meara's *Report of a Mission to the Ottawahs and Ojibwas on Lake Huron* [202]. Edward F. Wilson's *Missionary Work Among the Ojebway Indians* [270] provides later information on the same general region.

For Michigan, one of the earliest missionary publications is *Notices of Chippeway Converts* by William M. Ferry [99], the first Presbyterian missionary at Mackinac (on the straits between Lakes Michigan and Huron). In the Upper Peninsula, Ojibwa life in the region from Sault Sainte Marie west to Keeweenaw Bay was graphically described by John H. Pitezel in *Lights and Shades of Missionary Life* [211]. Pitezel also wrote a biography of one of his converts, entitled *Life of Reverend Peter Marksman, an Ojibwa Missionary* [212]. Marksman slipped from grace more than once during a career as missionary, interpreter, and surveyer.

Catholic missions were reintroduced in both the Lower and Upper Peninsulas of Michigan in the 1830s. A leading figure in this area was Father Frederick Baraga, who established stations among the Ottawas and Ojibwas of Little Traverse Bay, the Beaver Islands, Manistique, and on Keeweenaw Bay where a town bears his name. Baraga's trials and accomplishments are recorded in Father Chrysostom Verwyst's *Life and Labors of Rt. Rev. Frederick Baraga* [255]. For a particularly vivid narrative of life among the Keeweenaw Bay Ojibwas after the Civil War, read Joseph Raleigh Nelson's *Lady Unafraid* [200]. The "lady" in this biographical study was Nelson's mother who, at the age of seventeen, became Father Baraga's missionary neighbor at the Methodist station at the opposite side of Keeweenaw Bay.

Religious endeavors in the Saginaw Bay region of southeastern Michigan are described in Charles F. Luckhard's *Faith in the Forest: A True Story of Pioneer*

Lutheran Missionaries Laboring Among the Chippewa Indians in Michigan, 1833–1868 [186]. Lutheran activities are discussed by Albert Keiser, "The Work Among the Chippewas in Michigan and Minnesota" [162] and by William Gustave Polack, *Bringing Christ to the Ojibways in Michigan; A Story of the Mission Work of E. R. Baierlein, 1848–1853* [213].

Some especially helpful references on general mission work in Minnesota include: Henry B. Whipple, "Civilization and Christianization of the Ojibways of Minnesota" [267]; Joseph A. Gilfillan, "The Ojibways of Minnesota" [107]; James P. Schell, *In the Ojibway Country; A Story of Early Missions on the Minnesota Frontier* [234]; William H. Ketcham, "The Chippewa Missions of Minnesota" [165]; Father Alban Fruth, *A Century of Missionary Work Among the Red Lake Chippewa Indians, 1858–1958* [105]; Father George A. Belcourt, "Department of Hudson's Bay" [20] (which describes the regional Indian population as well as the pioneer Catholic mission of the Red River region on the western edge of Ojibwa country); and Nancy Woolworth, "The Grand Portage Mission: 1731–1965" [274].

Two men listed above merit special comment. Henry B. Whipple was the vigorous Episcopalian bishop who came to Minnesota in 1860 and acquired national influence in the post–Civil War Indian "reform" movement. Joseph A. Gilfillan publicized the Pillager Band's objections to the land sale that led to an armed confrontation at Leach Lake in 1898. His explanation of its causes was published as "The Minnesota Trouble" [106]. Another contemporary account of the same controversy is Francis Ellington Leupp's "The Protest of the Pillager Indians" [183]. Read Pauline Wold's "Some Recollections of the Leech Lake Uprising" [272] for a later view of the incident.

Regional Studies

This discussion of Ojibwa source material indicates that there has been no synthesis of Ojibwa history spanning the entire geographic range of loosely related communities. Literature is most extensive for the Ojibwas living in northern Minnesota and the adjacent Canadian border country. Supplementary coverage of other areas will be found in diverse publications. For example, Wisconsin is the principal focus of M. Carolissa Levi's *Chippewa Indians of Yesterday and Today* [184]. The region south of Lake Superior is treated by the observant German traveler Johann Georg Kohl in his *Kitchi-Gama* [169]. Kohl included a description of an annuity payment day in this work. Because there are so few Native American authors whose information extends back past the mid-nineteenth century, attention should be given to Andrew J. Blackbird, *History of the Ottawa and Chippewa Indians of Michigan* [28]. Blackbird was present at treaty councils, and the information he collected provided ammunition for his persistant protests to the federal government concerning the treatment of his people.

The history of the Ojibwas in southeastern Michigan — identified as the Saginaw, Swan Creek, and Black River bands — can be pieced together from well-written county histories: the anonymous *History of Genessee County* [133]; William Lee Jenks, *St. Clair County, Michigan, Its History and Its People* [151]; Michael A. Leeson, and Damon Clarke, *History of Saginaw County, Michigan* [181]; and James Cooke Mills, *History of Saginaw County* [192]. Nineteenth-century Ojibwa village sites (as well as more ancient mounds and burial grounds) are detailed in the large-scale maps of Wilbert B. Hinsdale's *Archaeological Atlas of Michigan* [131]. As a means of protecting burial grounds and other potential archaeological sites, locations are plotted with a known degree of error.

Anthropological Contributions

The study of Indian people has long been considered a special province of anthropologists. Publications by anthropologists dealing with the Ojibwas cover a broad range of subjects, including such material concerns as the use of tools and bark records; the construction of homes, canoes, and snow shoes; decorative basketry, wild rice gathering, and sugar making; and hunting and fishing skills. Also treated are the less tangible aspects of Ojibwa life: kinship and interpersonal relationships; diseases and cures; religion and secret societies; myths and legends; and individual personality characteristics and group social organization.

Among the anthropologists, the outstanding figure in Ojibwa studies has been A. Irving Hallowell, from whose extensive research a careful selection has been made. His collection of papers published as *Culture and Experience* [114] is virtually a theoretical textbook with accompanying illustrative examples from Ojibwa communities. These papers, or chapters, are principally based upon field work conducted between 1930 and 1940 among the northern Ojibwas living along the Berens River east of Lake Winnipeg. For purposes of comparison, Hallowell also discussed the different characteristics of the less remote Lac du Flambeau Ojibwas of northern Wisconsin, where he collected data mainly in 1946. In many of his essays, Hallowell's interpretation of Ojibwa behavior is heavily psychological in emphasis, containing some psychiatric analysis. Ethnohistorical backgrounds are provided for the two communities contrasted in this work. *Culture and Experience* offers a complete bibliography of earlier Hallowell publications.

Another major contributor to Ojibwa research is Frances Densmore, whose examination of customs, music, and plant use was first published between 1910 and 1929 in the Bureau of American Ethnology Bulletins (reprinted since 1970) [81, 84, 85]. Densmore is chiefly known as an authority on Indian music. It is fortunate that some of the songs she recorded have become available through the Library of Congress [88].

Any list of basic anthropological works on the Ojibwas should include two studies by Ruth Landes, *Ojibwa*

Sociology [176] and *The Ojibwa Woman* [177]. The latter utilizes the piecing together of recorded conversations to present a rather intimate view of the personal problems of women in Ojibwa society. Landes dealt with the challenging topic of the famed Indian secret society in *Ojibway Religion and the Midéwiwin* [178]. The classic discussion of this subject is Walter J. Hoffman, "The Midē'wiwin or 'Grand Medicine Society' of the Ojibwa" [139].

Two other anthropologists with long and diverse publication records are Sisters Bernard Coleman and Inez Hilger, both of whom have worked among the Ojibwas of northern Minnesota. The earliest Coleman study, "The Religion of the Ojibwas of Northern Minnesota" [64] highlights a single aspect of the culture. Her most recent effort is a comprehensive treatment of a single community, *Where the Water Stops: Fond du Lac Reservation* [67]. Hilger's outstanding contribution, *Chippewa Life and Its Cultural Background* [130] is recognized by present day reservation-reared Ojibwas as a valid interpretation of their own childhood experiences. For more informal statements, see the ten short articles by Fred K. Blessing published in *The Minnesota Archaeologist* in the 1950s [29–37]. These brief but specific presentations represent the data collected by Blessing during fifteen years of contact with the Minnesota Ojibwas.

Writing as an anthropologist-turned-ethnohistorian, Harold Hickerson has made significant additions to Ojibwa studies and to research methodology. His two leading publications are *The Southwestern Chippewa; An Ethnohistorical Study* [122] and *The Chippewa and Their Neighbors: A Study in Ethnohistory* [124]. From documentary and archival sources, Hickerson produced a particular study of the Ojibwas southwest of Lake Superior: he developed the concept of a well-defined "buffer zone" between regions occupied by the mutually hostile Sioux and Ojibwas in Wisconsin and Minnesota. On the basis on his own research, Hickerson questioned Hoffman's assumption that the midewiwin ceremony was part of Ojibwa pre-contact culture. Hickerson maintained, instead, that the ceremony was a post-contact development.

James G. E. Smith, a new contributor to the field, in his turn doubted Hickerson's emphasis on cooperative and communal elements as opposed to the often stressed "atomism" of Ojibwa clans and village groups. Smith's interpretation of regional Ojibwa cultural history through the 1970s is summarized in "Leadership among the Southwest Ojibwa" [241].

The degree to which traditional Ojibwa society has persisted, decayed, become acculturated or submerged in rural poverty, has been the subject of a debate among professional anthropologists, including Smith. The controversy was sparked by Bernard J. James's article, "Continuity and Emergence in Indian Poverty Culture" [149]. The latest round has begun with a challenging statement by Tim Roufs and a reply by James, "Myth in Method: More on Ojibwa Culture" [230]. Other participants in this continuing discussion will have their individual points of view presented in the forthcoming volume edited by J. Anthony Paredes, *Anishinabe: Six Studies of Modern Chippewas* [208]. The authors, in addition to the editor, are Michael A. Rynkiewish, Barbara Simon, Tim Roufs, Stuart Berde, and Gretel H. Pelto.

The Ojibwas also figure prominently in a current archaeological controversy over the relative positions of Ojibwas, Crees, and Assiniboines north of Lake Superior in the early sixteenth century. The case for the Ojibwas extending across the northern shore of Lake Superior was presented by J. V. Wright, "A Regional Examination of Ojibwa Culture History" [275].* Another hypothesis, that the Ojibwas extended only to Michipocten on the northwest shore, has been offered by Charles A. Bishop and M. Estellie Smith, "Early Historic Populations in Northwestern Ontario: Archaeological and Ethnohistorical Interpretations" [25]. Developments on this northwestern margin of Ojibwa country are vastly clari-

*Wright identified among other Ojibwa "subgroups" the Saulteurs, Missisaugas, Ottawas, and Potawatomies [275], pg. 7. This is in accord with the classification of Diamond Jenness, who noted four groups of Ojibwas: Ojibwas of Lake Superior, or Saulteurs; Missisaugas; Ottawas, or traders of Georgian Bay; and Potawatomies of the west side of Lake Huron. (See Jenness, Daimond. 1955. *The Indians of Canada.* 3d ed. National Museum of Canada, Bulletin:65, Anthropological Series:15. Ottawa: National Museum of Canada, pp. 277–83.) This Canadian perception of inter-tribal relations is not valid for the United States where Ojibwas, Ottawas, and Potawatomies have had separate tribal territories, although they have recognized earlier affiliations as "The Three Fires."

fied by a solid and original contribution from the field of cultural geography, Arthur J. Ray's *The Indians in the Fur Trade* [218]. This broad survey can be compared with the more specialized research of Bishop, *The Northern Ojibwa and the Fur Trade* [23]. Two other important publications concerning the Canadian Ojibwas are Robert William Dunning, *Social and Economic Change Among the Northern Ojibwa* [93] and Edward S. Rogers, *The Round Lake Ojibwa* [228].

Language and Tradition

In the field of linguistic anthropology a resurgence of academic interest accompanies the widespread enthusiasm among Ojibwa people for the acquisition of their traditional language. For example, Ojibwas at Mount Pleasant, Michigan, have acquired new copies of their original pocket-size hymnal, translated in the 1830s by the missionary Peter Jones [156]. This renewal of interest is reflected in the curricula of United States and Canadian universities. Bemidji State College offers a three-year sequence of Ojibwa classes. Basic courses are provided at the University of Minnesota, the College of Saint Scholastica at Duluth, Northern Michigan University at Marquette, and The University of Michigan at Ann Arbor. At the University of Western Ontario in London, language experts and psychologists have joined in a series of studies on the meaning of numbers to Ojibwa readers.

Modern linguistic research has produced three publications which provide a good starting point: the adult level instructional manual developed at the University of Minnesota by Delores Snook, et al., *Ojibwe Lessons, 1–5, 6–12* [243]; the recent report from the University of Western Ontario by J. Peter Denny and Lorraine Odjig, *A Semantically Organized List of Ojibway Numerical Classifiers* [80]; and the work which has become the basis for most current scholarly research on the Ojibwa language, Leonard Bloomfield's *Eastern Ojibwa: Grammatical Sketch, Texts, and Word List* [38] contains parallel texts in English and Ojibwa.

Two fundamental and still serviceable references in the field of linguistics are the first Ojibwa dictionary, compiled by Father Baraga [12] and his grammar [11]. A comprehensive bibliography of Ojibwa language materials is being assembled under the direction of John D. Nichols, Linguistic Coordinator for the Wisconsin Native American Languages Project of the Great Lakes Inter-Tribal Council, located at the University of Wisconsin at Milwaukee.

The current interest in language has prompted new publications of traditional history, biography, legends, poems, and stories — many by authors of Ojibwa heritage. In this area, Gerald Vizenor has made two contributions. *Anishenabe Adisokan* [258] presents "tales of the people" originally published in *The Progress,* the weekly newspaper of the White Earth Reservation during 1887 and 1888. His *Anishenabe Nagamon* [259] is a translation of Ojibwa songs or poems, each comprising a single visual image in form akin to Japanese poetry. Most anthologists of American Indian literature include selections from Ojibwa poetry as, for example, have Margot L. T. Astrov in *The Winged Serpent* [4] and Hattie Jones in *The Trees Stand Shining* [154]. Vizenor's *The Everlasting Sky* [257] is a contemporary portrait of the Ojibwas within a dual society — a traditional Native American culture straining within the often alien culture of the United States.

Among the more recent Canadian publications reflecting an Ojibwa outlook are: Norval Morriseau, *Legends of My People, the Great Ojibway* [195]; the accurate and absorbing biography written by James Redsky and edited by James R. Stevens, *Great Leader of the Ojibwa: Mis-quona-queb* [222]; and Norman Quill's *The Moons of Winter and Other Stories,* edited by Charles Fiero [215]. The latest Native American autobiography is John Rogers's *Red World and White; Memories of a Chippewa Boyhood* [229]. Older life stories, more historical than literary in their import, include: John Johnson or Enmegahbowh, *En-me-gah-bowh's Story; An Account of the Disturbances of the Chippewa Indians at Gull Lake in 1857 and Their Removal in 1868* [97] and John Smith, *Chief John Smith, A Leader of the Chippewa, Age 117 Years; His Life Story as Told By Himself* [242].

The Portrayal of Ojibwa Life

To bring to life the textual sources, special efforts have been made to locate pictorial records. The foremost production in the audio-visual field is the Minnesota Historical Society's *The Ojibwe; A History Resource Unit* [193]. Among the scenes and portraits of the *Unit* are reproductions of works by the Canadian artist Paul Kane and those of the American George Catlin, who recorded so many aspects of Indian life during extensive travels through the American West in 1831 and 1832. In Ojibwa country Catlin [57] painted views of Mackinac and Sault Sainte Marie, including a local canoe race, and detailed sketches of wigwams, snows shoes, and canoe instruction.* Catlin [58] also produced a series of drawings depicting an Ojibwa delegation on a European visit in 1845. That group of eleven was headed by a leading family from Lake Huron, accompanied by their two small children and a papoose (born during the journey).† During an 1845 trip from Toronto to Vancouver, Paul Kane made detailed portraits of Ojibwa subjects at Saugeen on the Lake Huron shore (at the base of the Bruce Peninsula), Manatoulin Island, Sault Sainte Marie, the Red River, and the Berens River at Lake Winnipeg.

*George Catlin, *Letters and Notes on the Manners, Customs, and Condition of the North American Indians* [57], pp. 137–41, plates 264 and 265.

†George Catlin, *Catlin's Notes of Eight Years' Travel and Residence in Europe, With His North American Indian Collection* [58], vol. 2, plate 18.

He illustrated an account of these experiences in *Wanderings of an Artist Among the Indians of North America* [159].

The most celebrated collection of American Indian portraits and biographies — reprinted at intervals throughout the twentieth century — is to be found in the *History of the Indian Tribes of North America* by Thomas L. McKenney and James Hall [188]. James D. Horan has recently provided a handy one-volume edition of a selection of the illustrations, *The McKenney-Hall Portrait Galley of American Indians* [140]. Horan's work includes eighteen Ojibwa portraits by Charles Bird King and his student George Cook. Some of these were painted during treaty negotiations at Fond du Lac in 1826, the remainder completed at Washington in 1827. The Ojibwa subjects include not only recognized leading men, but a woman and child, a widow, and a winsome young visitor to the nation's capital who became famous for her flawless French. McKenney also contributed a significant travel account, *Sketches of a Tour to the Lakes* [187].

The advent of photography vastly broadened the range of illustrated Ojibwa materials. Among the earliest such photographs are twenty-two pictures (taken at Pembina, Red Lake, Mille Lac, Lake Winnipeg, and some Wisconsin communities) listed in William Henry Jackson's *Descriptive Catalogue of Photographs of North American Indians* [146]. Jackson was a photographer who assisted in early government surveys. Another source of photographs is the National Anthropological Archives' microfiche collection (actually intended as an aid for authors seeking suitable book illustrations) entitled *North American Indians* [198]. Deserving of special mention is Charles Brill's brilliant contemporary photographic essay, *Indian and Free* [41]. Brill, a newspaper reporter, originally traveled to the Red Lake reservation in Minnesota for a feature story, but stayed on to compile a complete documentary record. In much the same vein, James Houston authored *Ojibwa Summer* [142].

Illustrations of special interest are often found in the periodical literature. One facet of an Ojibwa ceremony invoking the supernatural, a "shaking tent," is represented in an article by A. K. Black, "Shaking the Wigwam" [26]. Examples of the declining art of porcupine quill work are shown in Adelaide Leitch, "Porcupine Crafts" [182]. For a thorough understanding of Ojibwa crafts, artistic and utilitarian, Richard C. Schneider has offered an authentic "how to do it" volume, *Crafts of the American Indian, A Craftsman's Manual* [235].

Closely related to traditional dance forms, Ojibwa music is a key focus of artistic and religious expression. The best recent studies in the field of Ojibwa ethnomusicology are Thomas Vennum's introduction to the reprint of Densmore's *Chippewa Music* [81] and Gertrude P. Kurath's illustrated *Michigan Indian Festivals* [172]. New recordings include the Ponemah Chippewa Singers' "Chippewa" [61] and the Kingbird Family Singers' "Chippewa Grass Dance Songs" [62].

Treaties and Claims Cases

Since 1971, newspaper headlines and magazine articles have publicized the phrase "broken treaties" by focusing on legal proceedings arising out of the provisions of treaties between Indian nations and the federal government. The two indispensible reference works on this subject have achieved the status of classics; they are commonly cited as "Kappler" and "Royce." All treaties to which the Ojibwas were parties (and those in which Ojibwa bands were but mentioned) are indexed in *Indian Affairs, Laws and Treaties,* edited by Charles J. Kappler [160]. Treaty provisions touching upon land and reservations are abstracted and keyed to accompanying state maps in Charles C. Royce, *Indian Land Cessions in the United States* [231]. The Institute for the Development of Indian Law has published a set of forty-two Ojibwa treaties and four additional agreements, unfortunately lacking any editorial commentary [145]. Ojibwa treaties and land transactions in Canada are indexed in the government publication, *Indian Treaties and Surrenders, From 1680 to* [1903] [42].

Ojibwa claims against the United States, based upon treaty obligations, have been heard by the Indian Claims Commission established in 1946. Evidence given in these cases includes data brought together from previously uninvestigated sources. Legal testimony is often a biased presentation, but valuable information can be culled from the record. Seven volumes of decisions, findings of fact, reports of expert witnesses, and regional studies constitute one section of an American Indian ethnohistory series being published by Garland Press. These volumes present the Ojibwa researches of John C. Ewers [98]; Harold Hickerson [124–27]; Helen E. Knuth [168]; David B. Stout [245]; Helen Hornbeck Tanner [247]; Erminie Wheeler-Voegelin [265]; and Wheeler-Voegelin and Hickerson [266]. The series also makes available the Claims Commission's findings with respect to the Ojibwas [252].

Sources for Advanced Research

Extensive use has been made of correspondence printed in the *American State Papers* series, especially the two volumes on Indian affairs [251]. Scholars have been aided by numerous government publications: the *Annual Reports* of the Commissioners of Indian Affairs and the reports of congressional committees are but two of the many such sources of raw data. The United States National Archives and Records Service has prepared a select catalogue of their microfilm publications, *The American Indian* [253]. Often, correspondence with Indian agents, public figures, and the local citizenry has found its way into the official record through many channels — a good case in point is Alexander H. Ramsey's 1850 report [217], which contains some significant data. The Ojibwas are among the tribes studied by the Great Lakes – Ohio Valley Ethnohistory Research

Project, centered at Indiana University. The fourteen-year program, completed in 1969, was charged with the gathering of data for Indian claims cases. A tribally arranged archive assembled during that period is housed in a special collection at the Glenn A. Black Archaeological Laboratory on the Bloomington campus.

George Peter Murdock's contribution to the Human Relations Area Files, *Ethnographic Bibliography of North America,* has recently been revised by Timothy J. O'Leary [197]. Murdock, the standard reference for research on any Indian tribe, includes a substantial listing of source materials on the Ojibwas. A majority of the bibliographic items deal with the Minnesota and Wisconsin Ojibwas. Few publications cover the Eastern Ojibwas living in the Upper and Lower Peninsulas of Michigan and adjacent portions of the Ontario peninsula. Another characteristic of the scholarly literature is attention to the divisiveness of the Ojibwas and the role of small groups of close relatives. The essentially regional studies have not emphasized the ties between distant localities.*

*Ties have existed between geographically distant points, and some of these have yet to be emphasized in regional research studies. For example, the Ojibwas at Sault Sainte Marie in the late 1830s received a message from their people at the Bay of Quinte on Lake Ontario; the latter sought advice concerning a proposed tribal land grant for a new Methodist mission on nearby Grape Island. An 1840 report from Keeweenaw Bay on Lake Superior notes that a sister and brother have returned from a four year sojourn with relatives in Pembina, on the Red River near Winnipeg. In future research, such bits of data may become clues to understanding a network of vital inter-regional relationships among Ojibwa people.

The contemporary trend in non-technical publications is to stress the common bond uniting all people of Ojibwa heritage, the "Anishenabe." In line with this more recent development, the traditional history of the "Anishenabe" is being recovered with the aid of modern oral history techniques. The effective use of these new resources should contribute to a more balanced interpretation of many social phenomena and historical events already reported by outside investigators. A constructive approach to the whole field would feature a new appreciation of the value and validity of traditional history. The ultimate goal in the field of Ojibwa publications is unification and synthesis of regional studies through interdisciplinary research.

Recommended Works

For the Beginner

[41] Charles Brill, *Indian and Free; A Contemporary Portrait of Life on a Chippewa Reservation.*

[193] The Minnesota Historical Society, *The Ojibwe; A History Resource Unit.*

[227] Robert E. and Pat Ritzenthaler, *The Woodland Indians of the Western Great Lakes.*

[248] John Tanner, *A Narrative of the Captivity and Adventures of John Tanner.*

[257] Gerald R. Vizenor, *The Everlasting Sky.*

For a Basic Library Collection

[28] Andrew J. Blackbird, *History of the Ottawa and Chippewa Indians of Michigan.*

[61] The Ponemah Chippewa Singers, "Chippewa" [Recording].

[62] The Kingbird Family Singers, "Chippewa Grass Dance Songs" [Recording].

[114] A. Irving Hallowell, *Culture and Experience.*

[120] Alexander Henry, *Travels and Adventures in Canada and the Indian Territories.*

[124] Harold Hickerson, *The Chippewa and Their Neighbors: A Study in Ethnohistory.*

[130] Inez Hilger, *Chippewa Child Life and Its Cultural Background.*

[134] Fredrick W. Hodge, ed., *Handbook of American Indians North of Mexico.*

[184] M. Carolissa Levi, *Chippewa Indians of Yesterday and Today.*

[193] The Minnesota Historical Society, *The Ojibwe; A History Resource Unit.*

[199] Edward D. Neill, "History of the Ojibways, and Their Connection with Fur Traders Based Upon Official and Other Records."

[208] J. Anthony Paredes, ed., *Anishinabe: Six Studies of Modern Chippewas.*

[227] Robert E. and Pat Ritzenthaler, *The Woodland Indians of the Western Great Lakes.*

[248] John Tanner, *A Narrative of the Captivity and Adventures of John Tanner.*

[258] Gerald R. Vizenor, ed., *Anishenabe Adisokan; Tales of the People.*

[263] William W. Whipple, "History of the Ojibways Based upon Tradition and Oral Statements."

Bibliographical List

*Denotes items suitable for secondary school students

[1] American Scientific Corp. 1963. *Creation of New Industries on the Turtle Mountain Reservation for Turtle Mountain Agency, Belcourt, North Dakota.* Alexandria, Va.: American Scientific Corp.

[2] Armstrong, Benjamin G. 1892. *Early Life Among the Indians; Reminiscences from the Life of Benj. G. Armstrong. Treaties of 1835, 1837, 1842, and 1854. Habits and Customs of the Red Men . . . Incidents, Biographical Sketches, Battles, &c. Dictated to and Written by Thos. P. Wentworth . . .* Ashland, Wisc.: Press of A. W. Bowron.

[3] Arrow, Inc. 1970. *Industrial Parks in Indian Areas; A Guide for Businessmen.* Washington, D.C.: Arrow, Inc.

*[4] Astrov, Margot Luise Therese (Kröger), ed. 1946. *The Winged Serpent; An Anthology of American Indian Prose and Poetry.* New York: The John Day Co.

[5] Atwater, Caleb. 1831. *Remarks Made on a Tour to Prarie du Chien; Thence to Washington City, in 1829. By Caleb Atwater, Late Commissioner Employed by the United States to Negotiate with the Indians of the Upper Mississippi for the Purchase of*

Mineral Country . . . Columbus, Ohio: I. N. Whiting.

[6] Babbitt, Frances E. 1887. "Illustrative Notes Concerning the Minnesota Odjibwas." *Proceedings of the American Association for the Advancement of Science* 36:303–7. [Babbitt also authored a volume with this same title; no imprint information is available, save for 1887 being noted as the year of publication.]

[7] Babcock, Willoughby M. 1954. "The Minnesota Indian and His History." *The Minnesota Archaeologist* (July) 19:18–25.

[8] Baldwin, William W. 1957. "Social Problems of the Ojibwa Indians in the Collins Area in Northwestern Ontario." *Anthropologica* 5:51–123.

[9] Ball, A. E. 1894. "White Earth Consolidated Agency." In United States Census Office. *Report of Indians Taxed and Indians Not Taxed in the United States (excluding Alaska) at the Eleventh Census: 1890,* pp. 339–51. Washington, D.C.: Government Printing Office.

[10] Baner, John Gustav Runeskiold and Bellaire, John Ira. 1933. *Kitch-iti-ki-pi, the "Big Spring"; Wonderfully Beautiful (Namesakes)* . . . Manistique, Mich.: n.p.

Baraga, Friedrich.

[11] 1850. *A Theoretical and Practical Grammar of the Otchipwe Language, Spoken by the Chippewa Indians; Which is Also Spoken by the Algonquin, Otawa, and Potawatami Indians, With Little Difference. For the Use of Missionaries and Other Persons Living Among the Above Named Tribes.* Detroit: J. Fox. Rev. ed., ed. Albert Lacombe, Montreal: Beauchemain and Valois, 1878.

[12] 1853. *A Dictionary of the Otchipwe Language, Explained in English.* Cincinnati: Jos. A. Hemann. Rev. ed., ed. Albert Lacombe, Montreal: Beauchemain and Valois, 1878 and 1880. (Reprinted, Minneapolis: Ross and Haines, 1966.)

Barnouw, Victor

[13] 1949. "The Phantasy World of a Chippewa Woman." *Psychiatry* 12:67–76.

[14] 1950. *Acculturation and Personality among the Wisconsin Chippewa.* American Anthropology Association, Memoir: 72. Menasha, Wisc.: American Anthropological Association.

[15] 1954. "Reminiscences of a Chippewa Mide Priest." *The Wisconsin Archeologist* 35:83–112.

[16] 1955. "A Psychological Interpretation of a Chippewa Origin Legend." *Journal of American Folklore* 68:73–85; 211–23; and 341–55.

[17] 1960. "A Chippewa Mide Priest's Description of the Medicine Dance." *The Wisconsin Archeologist* 41:77–97.

[18] Barrett, Samuel Alfred. 1911. *The Dream Dance of the Chippewa and Menominee Indians of Northern Wisconsin.* Bulletin of the Public Museum of the City of Milwaukee:1, art. 4, pp. 251–406. Milwaukee, Wisc.: The Trustees.

[19] Beaulieu, T. H. 1900. *The Land Allotment Question of the Chippewas of the Mississippi on the White Earth Reservation, Minnesota* . . . Detroit, Minn.: G. D. Hamilton Print. [Not listed by *NUC,* this volume is available at the library of the Minnesota Historical Society.]

[20] Belcourt, George Antoine. 1872. "Department of Hudson's Bay," trans. Mrs. Letitia May. *Collections of the Minnesota Historical Society* 1:207–44. (Reprinted from an earlier publication of the Society.)

[21] Beltrami, Giacomo Constantino. 1828. *A Pilgrimage in Europe and America, Leading to the Discovery of the Sources of the Mississippi and Bloody River; With a Description of the Whole Course of the Former, and of the Ohio.* 2 vols. London: Hunt and Clarke.

[22] Bernard, M. 1929. "Religion and Magic among Cass Lake Ojibwa." *Primitive Man* 2:52–55.

[23] Bishop, Charles Aldrich. 1974. *The Northern Ojibwa and the Fur Trade; An Historical and Ecological Study*. Toronto: Holt, Rinehart and Winston of Canada.

Bishop, Charles Aldrich and M. Estellie Smith.

[24] 1970. "The Emergence of Hunting Territories Among the Northern Ojibwa." *Ethnology* 9: 1–15.

[25] 1975. "Early Historic Populations in Northwestern Ontario: Archaeological and Ethnohistorical Interpretations." *American Antiquity* 40: 54–63.

*[26] Black, A. K. 1934. "Shaking the Wigwam." *The Beaver* (Dec.) Outfit 265:13–34.

[27] Black, Mary. 1972. "Ojibwa Questioning Etiquette and Use of Ambiguity." *Studies in Linguistics* 23:13–29.

*[28] Blackbird, Andrew Jackson (Chief Mack-aw-de-be-nessy). 1887. *History of the Ottawa and Chippewa Indians of Michigan; A Grammar of the Language and Personal and Family History of the Author, by Andrew J. Blackbird, Late U. S. Interpreter* . . . Ypsilanti, Mich.: The Ypsilantian Job Printing House. (Reprinted, Petoskey, Mich.: Little Traverse Regional Historical Society, Inc., 1967?)

*[29] 1952. "The Physical Characteristics of Southern Ojibwa Woodcraft." *The Minnesota Archaeologist* (Oct.) 18:9–21.

*[30] 1954. "Some Observations on the Use of Bark by Southern Ojibwa Indians." *The Minnesota Archaeologist* (Oct.) 19:3–14.

*[31] 1956. "Some Uses of Bone, Horn, Claws and Teeth by Minnesota Ojibwa Indians." *The Minnesota Archaeologist* (July) 20:1–11.

*[32] 1956. "Contemporary Costuming of Minnesota Chippewa Indians." *The Minnesota Archaeologist* (Oct.) 20:1–8.

*[33] 1956. "An Exhibition of Mide Magic." *The Minnesota Archaeologist* (Oct.) 20:9–13.

[34] 1956. "Miscellany." *The Minnesota Archaeologist* (Oct.) 20:14–17.

[35] 1961. "Discovery of a Chippewa Peyote Cult in Minnesota." *The Minnesota Archaeologist* (Jan.) 23:1–8.

*[36] 1961. "Fasting and Dreams Among Minnesota Ojibway." *The Minnesota Archaeologist* (Jan.) 23:9–11.

*[37] 1961. "A Visit to an Ojibway Dream Dance." *The Minnesota Archaeologist* (Jan.) 23:12–16.

[38] Bloomfield, Leonard. 1957. *Eastern Ojibwa: Grammatical Sketch, Texts, and Word List.* Ann Arbor: University of Michigan Press.

[39] Boggs, Steven Taylor. 1958, "Culture Change and the Personality of Ojibwa Children." *American Anthropologist* 60:47–58.

*[40] Breck, James Lloyd. 1910. *Chippeway Pictures from the Territory of Minnesota, 1857 . . .* Hartford, Conn.: Church Missions Pub. Co.

*[41] Brill, Charles. 1974. *Indian and Free; A Contemporary Portrait of Life on a Chippewa Reservation.* Minneapolis: University of Minnesota Press.

[42] Brosius, Samuel Martin. 1901. *The Urgent Case of the Mille Lac Indians . . .* Indian Rights Association, Publication:59. Philadelphia: Indian Rights Association.

[43] Brown, Theodore T. 1930. "Plant Games and Toys of Chippewa Children." *The Wisconsin Archeologist* 9:185–86.

[44] Burns and Roe, Inc. 1964. *Mineral Resources Study: Indian Reservations, Minnesota and Wisconsin.* New York: Burns and Roe, Inc.

[45] Burton, Frederick Russell. 1909. *American Primitive Music, With Especial Attention to the Songs of the Ojibways . . .* New York: Moffat, Yard, and Co. (Reprinted, Port Washington, N.Y.: Kennikat Press, 1969.)

Bushnell, David Ives, Jr.

[46] 1905. "An Ojibway Ceremony." *American Anthropologist* 7:69–73.

[47] 1919. "Ojibway Habitations and Other Structures." In *Smithsonian Institution. Annual Report . . . 1917,* pp. 609–17. Washington, D.C.: Government Printing Office.

[48] 1940. "Sketches by Paul Kane in the Indian Country, 1845–1848." *Smithsonian Miscellaneous Collections* 99:1–25.

[49] Cadzow, Donald A. 1926. "Bark Records of the Bungi Midéwin Society." *Indian Notes* 3:123–34.

[50] Calkins, Hiram. 1855. "Indian Nomenclature of Northern Wisconsin, with a Sketch of the Manners and Customs of the Chippewa." *Collections of the State Historical Society of Wisconsin* 1:119–26. [The Calkins article was presented at the 1854 meeting of the Society.]

[51] Cameron, Duncan. 1890. "A Sketch of the Customs, Manners, Way of Living of the Natives in the Barren County About Nipigon." In *Les Bourgeois de la Compagnie du Nord-Quest; Récits de Voyages, Lettres et Rapports inédits relatifs au Nord-Quest Canadien . . . ,* ed. Louis François Rodrique Masson, 2 vols., vol. 2, pp. 237–300. Québec: A. Cote et Cie, 1889–90. [Biographical data is provided on pp. 231–35.] (Facsimile re-

print, New York: Antiquarian Press, Ltd., 1960.)

[52] Canada. 1905–12. *Indian Treaties and Surrenders, From 1680 to* [1903] . . . 3 vols. in 2. Ottawa: S. E. Dawson Print. (Reprinted, 3 vols., Coles Canadiana Collection, Toronto: Coles. Pub. Co.)

[53] Carver, Jonathan. 1778. *Travels Through the Interior Parts of North America, in the Years 1766, 1767, and 1768* . . . London: Printed for the Author. [Carver's work contains fictionalized accounts, but experts have yet to reach a consensus on what is and is not factual. The *Travels* should, therefore, be read with a critical eye and used with great caution.]

Casagrande, Joseph B.

[54] 1952. "Ojibwa Bear Ceremonialism: the Persistance of a Ritual Attitude." In *Proceedings of the 29th International Congress of Americanists,* 3 vols., vol. 2, *Acculturation in the Americas,* ed. Sol Tax, pp. 113–17. Chicago: University of Chicago Press.

[55] 1955. "John Mink, Ojibwa Informant." *The Wisconsin Archeologist* 36:106–28.

*[56] Castle, Beatrice Hanscom. 1974. *The Grand Island Story,* ed. James L. Carter. Marquette, Mich.: The John M. Longyear Research Library.

Catlin, George.

[57] 1842. *Letters and Notes on the Manners, Customs, and Condition of the North American Indians* . . . 3d ed. 2 vols. London: Tilt and Bogue. (Reprinted, Minneapolis: Ross and Haines, 1965 and 1970.)

[58] 1848. *Catlin's Notes of Eight Years' Travel and Residence in Europe, With His North American Indian Collection. With Anecdotes and Incidents of the Travels and Adventures of Three Parties of American Indians Whom He Introduced to the Courts of England, France, and Belgium.* 2nd ed. 2 vols. London: Printed for the Author.

Chamberlain, A. F.

[59] 1888. "Notes on the History, Customs, and Beliefs of the Mississagua Indians." *Journal of American Folklore* 1:150–60.

[60] 1889/90. "Tales of the Mississaguas." *Journal of American Folklore* 2:141–47 and 3:149–54.

*[61] "Chippewa, featuring the Ponemah Chippewa Singers." 1972. [Recording, #6082] Phoenix, Ariz.: Canyon Records.

*[62] "Chippewa Grass Dance Songs, featuring the Kingbird Family Singers." 1973. [Recording, #6106] Phoenix, Ariz.: Canyon Records.

[63] Coatsworth, Emerson S. 1957. *The Indians of Quetico, by Emerson S. Coatsworth from Field Notes*

and Research by Robert C. Dailey. Toronto: Published for the Quetico Foundation by the University of Toronto Press.

Coleman, Bernard, *Sister.*

[64] 1937. "The Religion of the Ojibwa of Northern Minnesota." *Primitive Man* 10:33–57.

[65] 1947. "Decorative Designs of the Ojibwa of Northern Minnesota." *Catholic University of America Anthropological Quarterly* 12:1–125.

[66] 1953. "The Ojibwa and the Wild Rice Problem." *Anthropological Quarterly* 1:79–88.

[67] 1967. *Where the Water Stops: Fond du Lac Reservation.* Duluth, Minn.: College of St. Scholastica.

*[68] Coleman, Bernard, *Sister*; Frogner, Ellen; and Eich, Estelle. 1962. *Ojibwa Myths and Legends.* Drawings by Ruth Maney. Minneapolis: Ross and Haines.

[69] Coleman, Bernard, *Sister*; LaBud, Verona, *Sister*; and Humphrey, John. 1968. *Old Crow Wing, History of a Village.* Duluth, Minn.: College of St. Scholastica.

[70] Colton, Calvin. 1833. *A Tour of the American Lakes, and Among the Indians of the North-West Territory in 1830: Disclosing the Character and Prospects of the Indian Race . . .* 2 vols. London: F.

Westley and A. H. Davis. (Reprinted, Port Washington, N.Y.: Kennikat Press, 1971.)

[71] Cooke, William R., *Mrs.* 1943. "A Michigan Indian Project." *Michigan History Magazine* 27:492–99.

[72] Cooper, John Montgomery. 1936. "Notes on the Ethnology of the Otchipwe of Lake of the Woods and Rainy Lake." *Catholic University of America Anthropological Series* 3:1–29.

[73] Copway, George [Ojibwa Chief]. *The Traditional History and Characteristic Sketches of the Ojibway Nation. By G. Copway, or Kah-ge-ga-gah-bowh, Chief of the Ojibway Nation.* London: C. Gilpin; Boston: B. F. Mussey and Co., 1851; and Boston: Sanborn, Carter, Brazin and Co., 1855. [Also issued under the title *Indian Life and Indian History* . . . Boston: A. Colby and Co., 1858 and 1860.]

[74] Coues, Elliott, ed. 1897. *New Light on the Early History of the Greater Northwest. The Manuscript Journals of Alexander Henry, Fur Trader of the Northwest Company, and of David Thompson, Official Geographer and Explorer of the Same Company, 1799–1814. Explorations and Adventures Among the Indians on the Red, Saskatchewan, Missouri and Columbia Rivers* . . . 3 vols. New York: F. P. Harper. (Reprinted, Minneapolis: Ross and Haines, 1965.)

[75] Crawford, Dean A.; Peterson, David L.; and Wurr, Virgil. 1967. *Minnesota Chippewa Indians; A Handbook for Teachers.* St. Paul, Minn.: Upper Midwest Regional Education Laboratory.

[76] Dally, Nathan. 1931. *Tracks and Trails; or, Incidents in the Life of a Minnesota Territorial Pioneer . . .* Walker, Minn.: The Cass County Pioneer.

[77] Davidson, John F. 1945. "Ojibwa Songs." *Journal of American Folklore* 58:303–5.

[78] Day, J. E. 1897. "Sketch of Peter Naw-gaw-nee, a Celebrated Indian of the Isabella County Reservation." *Collections and Researches made by the Michigan Pioneer and Historical Society* 27: 328–29.

[79] Delorme, David P. 1955. "History of the Turtle Mountain Band of the Chippewa Indians." *North Dakota History* 22:121–34.

[80] Denny, J. Peter and Odjig, Lorraine. 1972. *A Semantically Organized List of Ojibway Numerical Classifiers.* University of Western Ontario, Department of Psychology, Research Bulletin: 29. London, Ontario: University of Western Ontario, Department of Psychology.

Densmore, Frances.

[81] 1910–13. *Chippewa Music.* 2 vols. Smithsonian

Institution, Bureau of American Ethnology, Bulletin:45 and 53. Washington, D.C.: Government Printing Office. (Reprinted, Minneapolis: Ross and Haines, 1974.)

[82] 1919. "Material Culture Among the Chippewa." *Smithsonian Miscellaneous Collections*:70, pt. 2, pp. 114–18.

[83] 1920. "The Rhythm of Sioux and Chippewa Music." *Art and Archaeology* 9:59–67.

[84] 1928. "Uses of Plants by the Chippewa Indians." In *U. S. Bureau of American Ethnology. Forty-fourth Annual Report . . . 1926–27,* pp. 275–397. Washington, D.C.: U. S. Government Printing Office. (Reprinted as *How Indians Use Wild Plants for Food, Medicine, and Crafts,* New York: Dover Books, 1974.)

[85] 1929. *Chippewa Customs.* Smithsonian Institution, Bureau of American Ethnology, Bulletin:86. Washington, D.C.: U. S. Government Printing Office. (Reprinted, Minneapolis: Ross and Haines, 1971.)

[86] 1941. "The Native Art of the Chippewa." *American Anthropologist* 43:678–81.

[87] 1949. *A Study of Some Michigan Indians.* Museum of Anthropology, Ann Arbor, Anthropological Paper:1, pp. 1–49. Ann Arbor: University of Michigan Press.

*[88] 1950. "Songs of the Chippewa." [Recording] Recorded and ed. by U. S. Library of Congress, Music Division, Archive of American Folk Song. Washington, D.C.: U. S. Library of Congress, Music Division.

[89] Dewdney, Selwyn H. 1975. *The Sacred Scrolls of the Southern Ojibway.* Toronto: University of Toronto Press [as] Published for the Glenbow–Alberta Institute.

[90] Doty, James D. 1876. "Northern Wisconsin in 1820." *Collections of the State Historical Society of Wisconsin* 7:195–206.

[91] Ducatel, J. J. 1877. "A Fortnight Among the Chippewas of Lake Superior." In *The Indian Miscellany; Containing Papers on the History, Antiquities, Arts, Languages, Religions, Traditions and Superstitions of the American Aborigines; With Descriptions of Their Domestic Life, Manners, Customs, Traits, Amusements and Exploits; Travels and Adventures in the Indian Country; Incidents of Border Warfare; Missionary Relations, etc. . . . ,* ed. William Wallace Beach, pp. 361–75. Albany: J. Munsell.

Dunning, Robert William.

[92] 1959. "Rules of Residence and Ecology Among the Northern Ojibwa." *American Anthropologist* 6: 806–16.

[93] 1959. *Social and Economic Change Among the Northern Ojibwa.* Toronto: University of Toronto Press.

[94] Dustin, Fred. 1919. *The Saginaw Treaty of 1819 between General Louis Cass and the Chippewa Indians, Written for the Centennial Celebration of the Treaty, September 19th, 1919* . . . Saginaw, Mich.: Saginaw Pub. Co.

[95] Eastman, Charles A. 1911. "Life and Handicrafts of the Northern Ojibwas." *Southern Workman* 40:273–78.

[96] Elliott, Richard R. 1896. "The Chippewas of Lake Superior." *American Catholic Quarterly Review* 21:354–73.

[97] Enmegahbowh (John Johnson). 1904. *En-me-gah-bowh's Story; An Account of the Disturbances of the Chippewa Indians at Gull Lake in 1857, and Their Removal in 1868.* Minneapolis: Women's Auxillary, St. Barnabas Hospital.

[98] Ewers, John C. 1974. "Ethnological Report on the Chippewa Cree Tribe of the Rocky Boy Reservation, Montana, and the Little Shell Band of Indians." In *Chippewa Indians VI,* comp. and ed. David Agee Horr, pp. 9–182. American Indian Ethnohistory, North Central and Northeastern Indians. New York: Garland Press. [The Garland Series reprints many valuable and

often otherwise unobtainable studies. Pagination used here is that provided by Garland. David Horr's introductions are well worth the reader's attention.]

[99] Ferry, William Montague. 1833. *Notices of Chippeway Converts.* 3d ed. American Board of Commissioners for Foreign Missions, Missionary Paper:7. Boston: Crocker and Brewster, Prints.

[100] Flannery, Regina. 1940. "The Cultural Position of Spanish River Indians." *Primitive Man* 13: 1–25.

*[101] Foerster, John W. 1964. "An Indian Summer." *Canadian Geographical Journal* 68:157–63.

[102] Fox, Truman B. 1858. *History of Saginaw County, From the Year 1819 Down to the Present Time. Comp. From Authentic Records and Other Sources: Traditionary Accounts, Legends, Anecdotes, &c., With Valuable Statistics and Notes of Its Resources and General Information Concerning Its Advantages; Also, a Business Directory of Each of the Three Principal Towns of the County.* East Saginaw, Mich.: Enterprise Print. (Facsimile reprint, Mt. Pleasant, Mich.: Central Michigan University Press, 1963.)

Friedl, Ernestine.

[103] 1944. "A Note on Birchbark Transparencies." *American Anthropologist* 46:149–50.

[104] 1956. "Persistence in Chippewa Culture and Personality." *American Anthropologist* 58:814–25.

[105] Fruth, Alban (Bernard Fruth). 1958. *A Century of Missionary Work Among the Red Lake Chippewa Indians, 1858–1958*. Redlake, Minn.: St. Mary's Mission.

Gilfillan, Joseph A.

[106] 1898. "The Minnesota Trouble." In *Proceedings of the Sixteenth Annual Meeting of the Lake Mohonk Conference of Friends of the Indian,* ed. and rept. Isabel C. Barrows, pp. 18–27. [includes discussion]. [Philadelphia]: The Lake Mohonk Conference.

[107] 1901. "The Ojibways in Minnesota." *Collections of the Minnesota Historical Society* 9:55–128.

[108] 1902. "Ojibwa Characteristics." *Southern Workman* 31:260–62.

[109] Grant, Peter. 1890. "The Sauteux Indians About 1804." In *Les Bourgeois de la Compagnie du Nord-Ouest,* ed. Louis François Rodrique Masson, vol. 2, pp. 303–66. See [51].

[110] Greenman, Emerson F. 1940. "Chieftainship among Michigan Indians." *Michigan History* 24: 361–79.

*[111] Gringhuis, Richard H. [published as Dirk Gringhuis]. 1972. *Indian Costume at Mackinac:*

Seventeenth and Eighteenth Centuries. Michigan. Mackinac Island State Park Commission. Mackinac History, vol. 2, leaflet 1. Mackinac Island, Mich.: Mackinac Island State Park Commission.

Hallowell, Alfred Irving.

[112] 1939. "Sin, Sex and Sickness and Salteaux Belief." *British Journal of Medical Psychology* 18:191–97.

[113] 1946. "Concordance of Ojibwa Narratives in the Published Works of Henry R. Schoolcraft." *Journal of American Folklore* 59:136–53.

[114] 1955. *Culture and Experience.* Philadelphia: University of Pennsylvania Press. (Reprinted, New York: Schocken Books, 1967.)

[115] 1960. "Ojibway Ontology, Behavior and World View." In *Culture in History; Essays in Honor of Paul Radin,* ed. Stanley Diamond, pp. 19–52. New York: Columbia University Press for Brandeis University.

[116] 1963. "Ojibway World View and Disease." In *Man's Image in Medicine and Anthropology,* ed. Iago Galdston, pp. 258–315. Arden House Conference on Medicine and Anthropology, 1961. New York Academy of Medicine, Institute of Social and Historical Medicine, Monograph:4. New York: International Universities Press.

[117] 1966. "The Role of Dreams in Ojibwa Culture." In *The Dream and Human Societies,* eds. Gustave E. von Grunebaum and Roger Caillois, pp. 267–92. Berkeley: University of California Press.

[118] Hamilton, James Cleland. 1903. "The Algonquin Manabozho and Hiawatha." *Journal of American Folklore* 16:229–33.

[119] Hammond, J. Hugh. 1905. "The Ojibway of Lakes Huron and Simcoe." In Toronto. Ontario Provincial Museum. *Annual Archaeological Report 1904 being part of Appendix to the Report of the Minister of Education, Ontario,* pp. 71–76. Toronto: L. K. Cameron.

*[120] Henry, Alexander. 1809. *Travels and Adventures in Canada and the Indian Territories between the Years 1760 and 1776* . . . New York: I. Riley. (Reprinted, ed. Milo M. Quaife, Chicago: R. R. Donnelly and Co., 1921; Edmonton, Alberta: M. G. Hurtig, 1969.)

[121] Heritage, William. 1936. "Forestry, Past and Future, on Indian Reservations in Minnesota." *Journal of Forestry* 34:648–52.

Hickerson, Harold.

[122] 1962. *The Southwestern Chippewa; An Ethnohistorical Study.* American Anthropological Association, Memoir:92. Menasha, Wisc.: American Anthropological Association.

[123] 1967. *Land Tenure of the Rainy Lake Chippewa at the Beginning of the 19th Century*. Smithsonian Institution, Contributions to Anthropology:2, pt. 4. Washington, D.C.: Smithsonian Institution Press.

[124] 1970. *The Chippewa and Their Neighbors: A Study in Ethnohistory*. New York: Holt, Rinehart and Winston.

[125] 1974. "An Anthropological Report on the Indian Use and Occupancy of Royce Area 337, which was ceded to the United States by the Mississippi Bands, and the Pillager and Winnibigoshish Bands of Chippewa Indians under the Treaty of February 22, 1855." In *Chippewa Indians II,* comp. and ed. David Agee Horr, pp. 9–317. See [98].

[126] 1974. "An Anthropological Report on the Indian Use and Occupation of Royce Area 332, which was ceded to the United States by the Chippewa Indians of Lake Superior and the Mississippi under the Treaty of September 30, 1854 . . ." In *Chippewa Indians III,* comp. and ed. David Agee Horr, pp. 9–180. See [98].

[127] 1974. "An Anthropological Report on the Indian Occupancy of Area 242, which was ceded to the United States by the Chippewa Nation of Indians under the Treaty of July 29, 1837 . . ."

In *Chippewa Indians IV,* comp. and ed. David Agee Horr, pp. 9–253. See [98].

Hilger, Inez.

[128] 1936. "Chippewa Hunting and Fishing Customs." *The Minnesota Conservationist* 1:17–19.

[129] 1939. *A Social Study of One Hundred Fifty Chippewa Indian Families of the White Earth Reservation of Minnesota* . . . Washington, D.C.: Catholic University of America Press.

[130] 1951. *Chippewa Child Life and Its Cultural Background.* Smithsonian Institution, Bureau of American Ethnology, Bulletin:146. Washington, D.C.: U. S. Government Printing Office.

[131] Hinsdale, Wilbert B. 1931. *Archaeological Atlas of Michigan* . . . Ann Arbor: University of Michigan Press.

[132] Historical Records Survey. Minnesota. 1941. *The Report of the Chippewa Mission Archaeological Investigation* . . . [Reproduced from typewritten copy] St. Paul, Minn.: The Minnesota Historical Records Survey Projects.

[133] *History of Genesse County, Michigan With Illustrations and Biographical Sketches of Its Prominent Men and Pioneers.* 1879. Philadelphia: Everts and Abbott.

Hodge, Fredrick Webb, ed.

*[134] 1907–10. *Handbook of American Indians North of Mexico.* 2 vols. Smithsonian Institution, Bureau of American Ethnology, Bulletin:30. Washington, D.C.: Government Printing Office. (Reprinted, New York: Pageant Books, 1959.)

[135] 1913. *Handbook of the Indians of Canada. Published as an Appendix to the Tenth Report of the Geographic Board of Canada . . .* Ottawa: C. H. Parmelee. [This publication is a reprint of information extracted from the earlier two-volume *Handbook,* cited above. Hodge gave his assent to this project, but the actual work was directed by James White, who did an admirable job.]

Hoffman, Walter James.

[136] 1888. "Pictography and Shamanistic Rites of the Ojibwa." *American Anthropologist* 1:209–29.

[137] 1889. "Notes on Ojibwa Folk-Lore." *American Anthropologist* 2:215–23.

[138] 1890. "Remarks on Ojibwa Ball Play." *American Anthropologist* 3:133–35.

[139] 1891. "The Midē′ wiwin; or 'Grand Medicine Society' of the Ojibwa." In *U. S. Bureau of American Ethnology. Seventh Annual Report, 1885–86,* pp. 143–300. Washington, D.C.: Government Printing Office.

*[140] Horan, James D. 1972. *The McKenney–Hall Portrait Gallery of American Indians.* New York: Crown Pub. [Contains selections] See [188].

[141] Houghton, F. 1909. "Indian Village, Camp and Burial Sites on the Niagara Frontier." *Bulletin of the Buffalo Society of Natural Sciences* 9:261–62 and 263–374.

[142] Houston, James. 1972. *Ojibwa Summer.* Photographs by B. A. King. Barre, Mass.; Barre Pub.

[143] Hrdlička, Aleš (Alois Ferdinand). 1916. "Trip to the Chippewa Indians of Minnesota." *Smithsonian Miscellaneous Collections:*66, pt. 3, 263–74.

[144] Hubbard, Bela. 1887. *Memorials of a Half-Century in Michigan and the Lake Region . . .* New York and London: G. P. Putnam's Sons. (Reissued, New York and London: G. P. Putnam's Sons, 1888.)

*[145] Institute for the Development of Indian Law. 1974. *Treaties and Agreements of the Chippewa Indians.* [Introduction by Vine Deloria, Jr.] Washington, D.C.: Institute for the Development of Indian Law.

[146] Jackson, William Henry. 1877. *Descriptive Catalogue of Photographs of North American Indians.*

U. S. Geological and Geographical Survey of the Territories, Miscellaneous Publication:9. Washington, D.C.: Government Printing Office.

James, Bernard J.

[147] 1954. "Some Critical Observations Concerning Analyses of Chippewa 'Atomism' and Chippewa Personality." *American Anthropologist* 56:283–86.

[148] 1961. "Social-Psychological Dimensions of Ojibwa Acculturation." *American Anthropologist* 63:721–46.

[149] 1970. "Continuity and Emergence in Indian Poverty Culture." *Current Anthropology* 11:435–52.

[150] Jenks, Albert Ernest. 1900. "Wild Rice Gatherers of the Upper Lakes; A Study in American Primitive Economics." In *U. S. Bureau of Ethnology. Nineteenth Annual Report, 1897–98,* 2 pts. pt. 2, pp. 1013–1137. Washington, D.C.: Government Printing Office.

[151] Jenks, William Lee. 1912. *St. Clair County, Michigan, Its History and Its People; A Narrative Account of Its Historical Progress and Its Principal Interests* . . . 2 vols. Chicago and New York: The Lewis Pub. Co. [Volume 1 is germane to Ojibwa concerns.]

[152] Jenness, Diamond. 1935. *The Ojibwa Indians of Parry Island, Their Social and Religious Life . . .* National Museum of Canada, Bulletin:78, Anthropological Series:17. Ottawa: Department of Mines.

[153] Johnson, Frederick. 1929. "Notes on the Ojibwa and the Potawatomi of the Parry Island Reservation, Ontario." *Indian Notes* 6:193–216.

*[154] Jones, Hattie, comp. 1971. *The Trees Stand Shining; Poetry of the North American Indian.* Paintings by Robert Andrew Parker. New York: Dial Press.

[155] Jones, Peter [Ojibwa Chief]. 1861. *History of the Ojebway Indians; With Especial Reference to Their Conversion to Christianity. By Rev. Peter Jones, (Kahkewaquonaby), Indian Missionary . . .* London: A. W. Bennett. (Reissued, London: A. W. Bennett, 1864.)

[156] Jones, Peter [Ojibwa Chief], trans. 1840. *A Collection of Chippeway and English Hymns for the Use of the Native Indians. Translated by Peter Jones . . . To Which Are Added a Few Hymns Translated by Rev. James Evans and George Henry . . .* Toronto: Printed for the Translator. [Containing English and Ojibwa on facing pages, this version is based on the Jones 1829 ed., New York: Printed at the Conference Office by J. Collord. This work was

reprinted and reissued numerous times, often under various titles. James Evans and George Henry are frequently referenced as joint translators.] (Reprinted, from an 1847 Toronto ed., Ann Arbor: University Microfilms, 1969.)

[157] Jones, Volney H. 1936. "Some Chippewa and Ottawa Uses of Sweetgrass." *Papers of the Michigan Academy of Science, Arts and Letters for 1935* 21:21–31.

*[158] Jones, William. 1916. "Ojibwa Tales from North Shore of Lake Superior." *Journal of American Folklore* 29:368–91.

[159] Kane, Paul. 1859. *Wanderings of an Artist Among the Indians of North America from Canada to Vancouver's Island and Oregon, Through the Hudson's Bay Company's Territory and Back Again* . . . London: Longman, Brown, Green, Longmans and Roberts. (Reprinted, ed. J. W. Garvin, Toronto: The Radisson Society of Canada, 1925.)

[160] Kappler, Charles Joseph, comp. and ed. 1904. *Indian Affairs. Laws and Treaties* . . . 2 vols. Volume 2: *Treaties.* Washington, D.C.: U. S. Government Printing Office. (Volume 2 reprinted as *Indian Treaties, 1778–1883,* New York: Interland Pub., 1972.)

[161] Keating, William Hypolitus. 1824. *Narrative of*

an Expedition to the Source of St. Peter's River, Lake Winnepeek, Lake of the Woods, &c. &c. Performed in the Year 1823, By Order of the Hon. J. C. Calhoun, Secretary of War, Under the Command of Stephen H. Long, Major, U. S. T. E. *Comp. From the Notes of Major Long, Messrs. Say, Keating, & Calhoun . . .* 2 vols. Philadelphia: H. C. Carey and I. Lea. (Reprinted, London: G. B. Whittaker, 1825. Also appears later under the title *Travels in the Interior of North America . . .*, 2 vols., London: G. B. Whittaker, 1828.)

[162] Keiser, Albert. 1922. "The Work among the Chippewas in Michigan and Minnesota." In *Lutheran Mission Work among the American Indians,* pp. 55–94. Minneapolis: Augsburg Pub. House.

Kelton, Dwight H.

[163] 1888. *Indian Names of Places Near the Great Lakes . . . Vol. I.* Detroit: Detroit Free Press Print. Co.

[164] 1889. *Indian Names and History of the Sault Ste. Marie Canal . . .* Detroit: Detroit Free Press Print. Co.

[165] Ketcham, William H. 1920. "The Chippewa Missions of Minnesota." *The Indian Sentinel* 2:161–64.

Kinietz, William Vernon.

*[166] 1940. *Indian Tribes of the Western Great Lakes, 1615–1760.* University of Michigan, Museum of Anthropology, Occasional Contributions:10. Ann Arbor: University of Michigan Press. (Reprinted, Ann Arbor: University of Michigan Press, 1965.)

*[167] 1947. *Chippewa Village; The Story of Katikitegon.* Cranbrook Institute of Science, Bulletin:25. Bloomfield Hills, Mich.: Cranbrook Institute of Science.

[168] Knuth, Helen E. 1974. "Economic and Historical Background of Northeastern Minnesota Lands Ceded by Chippewa Indians of Lake Superior September 30, 1854, Royce Area 332, For Valuation as of January 10, 1855 (Date of Ratification) . . ." In *Chippewa Indians III,* comp. and ed. David Agee Horr, pp. 181–295. See [98].

[169] Kohl, Johann Georg. 1860. *Kitchi-Gami. Wanderings Round Lake Superior . . . ,* trans. Lascelles Wraxall. London: Chapman and Hall. [Wraxall omitted considerable information. For a complete account of these travels, see Kohl's *Kitschi-Gami; oder, Erzählungen vom Obern See. Ein Beitrag Zur Charakteristik der amerikanischen Indianer . . . ,* 2 vols. in 1, Bremen: C.

Schünemann, 1859.]

[170] Kuhm, Herbert W. 1952. "Indian Place Names in Wisconsin." *The Wisconsin Archeologist* 33: 1–157.

Kurath, Gertrude Prokosch.

[171] 1954. "Chippewa Sacred Songs in Religious Metamorphosis." *Scientific Monthly* 79:311–17.

*[172] 1966. *Michigan Indian Festivals.* Ann Arbor, Mich.: Ann Arbor Pub.

*[173] Laidlaw, George E. 1915. "Ojibwa Myths and Tales." In Toronto. Ontario Provincial Museum. *Twenty-Seventh Annual Archaeological Report 1915 being part of Appendix to the Report of the Minister of Education, Ontario,* pp. 71–90. Toronto: A. T. Wilgress. [For further examples of myths and legends published in this serial, see also: 1914, pp. 77–9; 1916, pp. 84–92; 1918, pp. 74–110; 1920, pp. 66–85; 1921, pp. 84–99; and 1924, pp. 34–80.]

[174] Lajeunesse, Ernest J., ed. 1960. *The Windsor Border Region, Canada's Southernmost Frontier; A Collection of Documents.* Toronto: The Champlain Society. [Texts in English and French.]

Landes, Ruth.

[175] 1937. "The Ojibwa of Canada." In *Cooperation and Competition among Primitive Peoples,* ed. Mar-

garet Mead, pp. 87–126. New York: McGraw–Hill.

[176] 1937. *Ojibwa Sociology.* Columbia University Contributions to Anthropology:29. New York: Columbia University Press.

[177] 1938. *The Ojibwa Woman.* Columbia University Contributions to Anthropology:31. New York: Columbia University Press. (Reprinted, New York: AMS Press, 1969, and New York: W. W. Norton and Co., 1971.)

[178] 1968. *Ojibway Religion and the Midéwiwin.* Madison: University of Wisconsin Press.

[179] Lathrop, Stanley Edwards. 1905. *A Historical Sketch of the "Old Mission," and Its Missionaries to the Ojibway Indians, on Madeline Island, Lake Superior, Wisconsin . . .* Ashland, Wisc.: The Author.

[180] Le Roy de la Potherie, Claude-Charles [published as Claude Charles Le Roy, Bacqueville de la Potherie]. 1911–12. "History of the Savage Peoples Who Are Allies of New France." In *The Indian Tribes of the Upper Mississippi Valley and Region of the Great Lakes as Described by Nicolas Perrot, French Commandant in the Northwest; Bacqueville de la Potherie, French Royal Commissioner to Canada; Morrell Marston, American Army Officer; and Thomas Forsyth, United States*

Agent at Fort Armstrong . . . , ed. and trans. Emma Helen Blair, 2 vols.; vol. 1, pp. 273–372 and vol. 2, pp. 12–136. Cleveland: The Arthur H. Clark Co.

[181] Leeson, Michael A. and Clarke, Damon. 1881. *History of Saginaw County, Michigan; Together with Sketches of Its Cities, Villages and Townships, Educational, Religious, Civil, Military, and Political History; Portraits of its Prominent Persons and Biographies of Representative Citizens.* Chicago: Chas. C. Chapman and Co. [Ojibwa materials may be found on pp. 117–40.]

[182] Leitch, Adelaide. 1955. "Porcupine Crafts." *Canadian Geographical Journal* 51:128–29.

[183] Leupp, Francis Ellington. 1898. "The Protest of the Pillager Indians." *The Forum* 26:471–84. [In 1930 the publication was renamed *Forum and Century.*]

*[184] Levi, M. Carolissa. 1956. *Chippewa Indians of Yesterday and Today.* New York: Pageant Press.

[185] Long, John. 1791. *Voyages and Travels of an Indian Interpreter and Trader, Describing the Manners and Customs of the North American Indians; With an Account of the Posts Situated on the River Saint Laurence, Lake Ontario, &c. To Which is Added a Vocabulary of the Chippeway Language . . . a List of Words in the Iroquois, Mehegan, Shawnee, and Es-*

quimeaux Tongues, and a Table Shewing the Analogy Between the Algonkin and Chippeway Languages . . . London: Printed for the Author. (Reprinted, ed. Milo M. Quaife, Chicago: R. R. Donnelly and Sons, 1927.)

[186] Luckhard, Charles F. 1952. *Faith in the Forest: A True Story of Pioneer Lutheran Missionaries Laboring Among the Chippewa Indians in Michigan, 1833–1868.* Sebewaing, Mich.: n.p.

[187] McKenney, Thomas Loraine. 1827. *Sketches of a Tour to the Lakes, of the Character and Customs of the Chippeway Indians, and of Incidents Connected With the Treaty of Fond du Lac . . . Also, a Vocabulary of the Algic, or Chippeway Language, Formed in Part, and as Far as It Goes, Upon the Basis of One Furnished By . . . A. Gallatin . . .* Baltimore: F. Lucas, Jun'r. (Reprinted, with introduction by Herman Viola, Barre, Mass.: Imprint Society, 1972.)

[188] McKenney, Thomas Lorraine and Hall, James. 1836–44. *History of the Indian Tribes of North America, With Biographical Sketches and Anecdotes of the Principal Chiefs. Embellished With One Hundred and Twenty Portraits, From the Indian Gallery in the Department of War, at Washington . . .* 3 vols. Philadephia: E. C. Biddle. (Reprinted, ed. Frederick Webb Hodge, 3 vols., vol. 2 eds. Hodge and David I. Bushnell, Jr., Edinburgh: J. Grant,

1933–34; reprinted, Totowa, N.J.: Rowman and Littlefield, 1972.) [The McKenney–Hall work was reprinted and reissued numerous times throughout the nineteenth century. The text underwent some revision and enlargement, but the earlier editions are specially valuable for the magnificent plates. An 1836–38 two-volume edition has been recorded, but this contains only sixty illustrations.] See [140].

[189] Mason, Philip Parker, ed. 1958. *Expedition to Lake Itasca; The Discovery of the Source of the Mississippi.* East Lansing: Michigan State University Press. [Annotated edition of Schoolcraft's 1834 *Narrative* . . .] See [237].

[190] Mekeel, Haviland Scudder. 1937. *Report on Michigan Indians.* n.p.

[191] Merwin, B. W. 1916. "Some Ojibway Buffalo Robes." *Museum Journal of the University of Pennsylvania* 7:93–96. [Unpaginated plates precede and follow the text.]

[192] Mills, James Cooke. 1918. *History of Saginaw County, Michigan; Historical, Commercial, Biographical, Profusely Illustrated With Portraits of Early Pioneers, Rare Pictures and Scenes of Olden Times, and Portraits of Representative Citizens of Today* . . . 2 vols. Saginaw, Mich.: Seemann and

Peters. [Volume 1, pp. 21–65 and pp. 117–40 contains material relating to the Ojibwas.]

*[193] The Minnesota Historical Society. 1973. *The Ojibwe; A History Resource Unit.* Produced by the Ojibwe Curriculum Committee, Indian Studies Department, University of Minnesota; and the Educational Services Division, Minnesota Historical Society. St. Paul, Minn.: The Minnesota Historical Society. [The *Unit* constitutes three interrelated parts: "Filmstrips and Records"; "Booklets"; and "Resources." The materials are so arranged as to allow for both elementary and secondary school presentation; the components are attractively boxed to facilitate handling and storage. The Newberry Library's Center for the History of the American Indian has used *The Ojibwe* as a model of curriculum development for secondary school teachers interning at the Center's Summer Institute in American Indian History. Educators and laymen alike will benefit from exposure to this well designed package.]

*[194] Mooney, James and Thomas, Cyrus. 1907. "Chippewa" and "Missisauga." In *Handbook of American Indians*, ed. Frederick Webb Hodge, 2 vols., vol. 1, pp. 277–81 and pp. 909–10, respectively. See [134].

*[195] Morriseau, Norval. 1965. *Legends of My People,*

the Great Ojibway, ed. Selwyn H. Dewdney. Toronto: Ryerson Press.

[196] Morse, Richard E. 1856. "The Chippewas of Lake Superior." *Collections of the State Historical Society of Wisconsin* 3:338–69.

[197] Murdock, George Peter. 1975. *Ethnographic Bibliography of North America.* 4th ed., rev. by Timothy J. O'Leary. 5 vols. New Haven: Human Relations Area File Press.

*[198] National Museum of Natural History. National Anthropological Archives. 1974. *North American Indians. Photographs from the National Anthropological Archives, Smithsonian Institution,* comp. Herman Viola. [Microfiche ed., containing 52 cards] Chicago: University of Chicago Press.

*[199] Neill, Edward Duffield. 1885. "History of the Ojibways, and Their Connection with Fur Traders Based Upon Official and Other Records." *Collections of the Minnesota Historical Society* 5:395–510.

*[200] Nelson, Joseph Raleigh. 1951. *Lady Unafraid.* Caldwell, Idaho: Caxton Printers.

[201] Nichols, *Mrs.* Frances Sellman (Gaither), ed. 1954. *Index to Schoolcraft's Indian Tribes of the United States.* Smithsonian Institution, Bureau of American Ethnology, Bulletin:152. Washington, D.C.: U. S. Government Printing Office.

O'Meara, Frederick Augustus.

[202] 1846. *Report of a Mission to the Ottahwahs and Ojibwas, on Lake Huron* . . . Missions to the Heathen. No. VI. London: The Society for the Propagation of the Gospel.

[203] 1846. *Second Report of a Mission to the Ottahwahs and Ojibwas, on Lake Huron* . . . Missions to the Heathen. No. XIII. London: The Society for the Propagation of the Gospel. [Often appears bound with *Report* listed above.]

Orr, Rowland B.

[204] 1915. "The Mississaugas." In Toronto. Ontario Provincial Museum. *Twenty-Seventh Annual Archaeological Report 1915 being part of Appendix to the Report of the Minister of Education, Ontario,* pp. 7–19. Toronto: A. T. Wilgress.

[205] 1918. "The Chippewas." In Toronto. Ontario Provincial Museum. *Thirtieth Annual Archaeological Report 1918 being part of Appendix to the Report of the Minister of Education,* Ontario, pp. 9–24. Toronto: A. T. Wilgress.

*[206] Osborn, Chase Salmon and Osborn, Stella Brunt [published as Stellanova Osborn]. 1942. *Schoolcraft, Longfellow, Hiawatha.* Lancaster, Pa.: The Jaques Cattell Press.

*[207] Owl, Frell M. 1952. "Seven Chiefs Rule the Red

Lake." *The American Indian* (Summer) 6:3–12.

[208] Paredes, J. Anthony, ed. Forthcoming. *Anishinabe: Six Studies of Modern Chippewas.* Gainesville: University Presses of Florida. [Title may vary slightly, as this represents the publisher's tentative choice.]

[209] Perrot, Nicholas. 1911. "Memoir on the Manners, Customs, and Religion of the Savages of North America." In *The Indian Tribes of the Upper Mississippi Valley and Region of the Great Lakes,* ed. Emma Helen Blair, vol. 1, pp. 23–272. See [180].

[210] Pike, Zebulon Montgomery. 1895. *The Expeditions of Zebulon Montgomery Pike, to the Headwaters of the Mississippi River, Through Louisana Territory, and in New Spain, During the Years 1805–6–7. A New Ed., Now First Reprinted in Full From the Original of 1810, With Copious Critical Commentary, Memoir of Pike . . . and Complete Index . . . ,* ed. Elliot Coues. 3 vols. New York: F. P. Harper.

Pitezel, John H.

[211] 1857. *Lights and Shades of Missionary Life: Containing Travels, Sketches, Incidents and Missionary Efforts, During Nine Years Spent in the Region of Lake Superior . . .* Cincinnati: Western Book Concern, for the Author. (Reprinted, Cincinnati: Western Book Concern, 1859, 1860, 1861; with Supplement, New York and Philadelphia: Phil-

lips and Hunt, 1883; and Cincinnati: Walden and Stowe, 1883.)

[212] 1901. *Life of Reverend Peter Marksman, an Ojibwa Missionary; Illustrating the Triumphs of the Gospel Among Ojibwa Indians . . .* Cincinnati: Western Book Concern, for the Author.

[213] Polack, William Gustave. 1927. *Bringing Christ to the Ojibways in Michigan; A Story of the Mission Work of E. R. Baierlein, 1848–1853.* New York: n.p. (Reprinted, St. Louis, Mo.: Concordia Pub. House, n.d.)

[214] Pruitt, O. J. 1955/57. "A Tribe of Chippewa Indians." *Annals of Iowa* (3d ser.) 33: 295–97.

*[215] Quill, Norman. 1965. *The Moons of Winter and Other Stories,* ed. Charles E. Fiero. Red Lake, Ontario: Northern Light Gospel Mission.

[216] Radin, Paul. 1928. "Ecological Notes on the Ojibwa of Southeastern Ontario." *American Anthropologist* 30:659–68.

[217] Ramsey, Alexander H. 1850. "[Report] No. 1. Minnesota Superintendency; St. Paul's Oct. 13th 1849." In *Annual Report of the Commissioner of Indian Affairs . . . 1849–50,* pp. 68–99. Washington, D.C.: Gideon and Co. [The document gives rather extensive coverage to the Ojibwas and neighboring tribes. Ramsey later

negotiated an Indian treaty (signed 23 July 1851), and the ensuing transfer of funds embroiled him in a hotly debated controversy. For an in-depth account of those charges, see United States Congress, Senate. 1854. "Report of the Commissioners, appointed By the President of the United States, to investigate the official conduct of Alexander H. Ramsey, late governor of Minnesota Territory . . ." Thirty-third Congress, 1st session. Ex. Doc. No. 61. Washington, D.C.: Beverley Tucker, Senate Print.]

*[218] Ray, Arthur J. 1974. *Indians in the Fur Trade: Their Role as Trappers, Hunters, and Middlemen in the Lands Southwest of Hudson Bay 1660–1870.* Toronto: University of Toronto Press.

Reagan, Albert B.

[219] 1923. "Rainy Lakes Indians." *The Wisconsin Archeologist* 2:140–47.

[220] 1924. "The Bois Fort Chippewa." *The Wisconsin Archeologist* 3:101–32.

[221] 1927. "Picture Writings of the Chippewa Indians." *The Wisconsin Archeologist* 6:80–83.

*[222] Redsky, James. 1972. *Great Leader of the Ojibwa: Mis-quona-queb,* ed. James R. Stevens. Toronto: McClelland and Stewart.

[223] Riggs, Stephen R. 1894. "Protestant Missions in the Northwest." *Collections of the Minnesota Historical Society* 6:117–88.

[224] Ringland, Mabel Crews. 1933. "Indian Handicrafts of Algoma." *Canadian Geographical Journal* 6:185–201.

Ritzenthaler, Robert Eugene.

*[225] 1947. "The Chippewa Indian Method of Securing the Tanning Deerskin." *The Wisconsin Archeologist* 28:6–13.

[226] 1963. "Primitive Therapeutic Practices Among the Wisconsin Chippewa." In *Man's Image in Medicine and Anthropology*, ed. Iago Galdston, pp. 316–34. See [116].

*[227] Ritzenthaler, Robert Eugene and Ritzenthaler, Pat. 1970. *The Woodland Indians of the Western Great Lakes.* American Museum Science Book B 21. Garden City, N.Y.: Published for the American Museum of Natural History by the Natural History Press.

[228] Rogers, Edward S. 1962. *The Round Lake Ojibwa.* University of Toronto, Royal Ontario Museum, Art and Archaeology Division, Occasional Paper: 5. Toronto: Ontario Department of Lands and Forests for the Royal Ontario Museum.

*[229] Rogers, John [Ojibwa Chief]. 1974. *Red World*

and White; Memories of a Chippewa Boyhood, by John Rogers (Chief Snow Cloud). New ed. The Civilization of the American Indian Series:126. Norman: University of Oklahoma Press. (First published as *A Chippewa Speaks,* 1957.)

[230] Roufs, Tim. 1974. "Myth in Method: More on Ojibwa Culture" and Bernard J. James, "Reply." *Current Anthropology* 15:307–10.

[231] Royce, Charles C. 1899. "Indian Land Cessions in the United States." In *U. S. Bureau of American Ethnology. Eighteenth Annual Report 1896–97,* 2 pts., pt. 2, pp. 521–997. Washington, D.C.: Government Printing Office. [Includes an introduction by Cyrus Thomas.]

[232] Ruffee, Charles A. 1875. *Report of the Condition of the Chippewas of Minnesota.* St. Paul, Minn.: The Pioneer Co. Print.

[233] Sagatoo, Mary A. (Henderson) Cabay. 1897. *Wah Sash Kah Moqua; or, Thirty-three Years Among the Indians.* Boston: C. A. White Co.

[234] Schell, James Peery. 1911. *In the Ojibway Country: A Story of Early Missions on the Minnesota Frontier.* Walhalla, N.D.: C. E. Lee.

*[235] Schneider, Richard C. 1972. *Crafts of the North American Indians; A Craftsman's Manual.* Stevens Point, Wisc.: The Author. (Reprinted, New York: Van Nostrand Reinhold Co., 1974.)

Schoolcraft, Henry Rowe.

[236] 1821. *Narrative Journal of Travels Through the Northwestern Regions of the United States; Extending From Detroit Northwest Through the Great Chain of American Lakes, to the Sources of the Mississippi River.* Albany: E. E. Hosford.

[237] 1834. *Narrative of an Expedition Through the Upper Mississippi to Itasca Lake, the Actual Source of This River; Embracing an Exploratory Trip Through the St. Croix and Burntwood (or Brule) Rivers: In 1832.* New York: Harper and Bros. See [189].

[238] 1839. *Algic Researches, Comprising Inquiries Respecting the Mental Characteristics of the North American Indians . . .* 2 vols. New York: Harper and Bros.

[239] 1851. *Personal Memoirs of a Residence of Thirty Years with the Indian Tribes on the American Frontiers, with Brief Notices of Passing Events, Facts, and Opinions, A.D. 1812 to A.D. 1842.* Philadelphia: Lippincott, Grambo, and Co.

[240] 1851–57. *Historical and Statistical Information Respecting the History, Conditions and Prospects of the Indian Tribes of the United States; collected and prepared under the direction of the Bureau of Indian Affairs per Act of Congress of March 3d, 1847.* Illustrated by S. Eastman. 6 vols. Philadelphia: Lippincott, Grambo and Co. [Reprinted and re-

issued numerous times under various titles, all of which contain substantially similar information.]

[241] Smith, James G. E. 1973. *Leadership Among the Southwestern Ojibwa.* National Museums of Canada, Publications in Ethnology:7. Ottawa: National Museums of Canada.

[242] Smith, John. [1919?] *Chief John Smith, A Leader of the Chippewa, Age 117 Years. His Life as Told by Himself. Being the Life Story of Chief John Smith as Narrated by Himself and Interpreted by His Adopted Son, Thomas E. Smith.* Walker, Minn.: The Cass County Pioneer.

[243] Snook, Delores, et al. 1972. *Ojibwe Lessons 1–5; 6–12.* Minneapolis: University of Minnesota, Department of American Indian Studies.

[244] Steinbring, J. 1964/65. "Culture Change Among the Northern Ojibwa." *Papers of the Historical and Scientific Society of Manitoba* (No. 21) 3:13–24.

[245] Stout, David B. 1974. "Ethnohistorical Report on Royce Area 111 (Michigan)." In *Chippewa Indians V,* comp. and ed. David Agee Horr, pp. 87–132. [Treats the Saginaw Ojibwas, among others.] See [98].

[246] Stowe, Gerald C. 1940. "Plants Used by the

Chippewa." *The Wisconsin Archeologist* 21:8–13.

[247] Tanner, Helen Hornbeck. 1974. "The Chippewa of Eastern Lower Michigan." In *Chippewa Indians V,* comp. and ed. David Agee Horr, pp. 347–77. See [98].

*[248] Tanner, John. 1830. *A Narrative of the Captivity and Adventures of John Tanner (U. S. Interpreter at the Saut de Ste. Marie) During Thirty Years Residence Among the Indians in the Interior of North America,* ed. Edwin James. New York: G. and C. and H. Carvill. (Reprinted, Minneapolis: Ross and Haines, 1956.)

[249] Thompson, David. 1916. *David Thompson's Narrative of His Explorations in Western America, 1784–1812,* ed. Joseph Burr Tyrrell. Toronto: The Champlain Society. (Facsimile ed., New York: Greenwood Press, 1968.)

[250] Thwaites, Reuben Gold, ed. 1896–1901. *The Jesuit Relations and Allied Documents: Travels and Explorations of the Jesuit Missionaries in New France, 1610–1791.* 73 vols. Cleveland: The Arthur H. Clark Co. (Reprinted, 73 vols. in 36, New York: Pageant Book Co., 1959.)

[251] United States Congress. 1832–34. *American State Papers. Indian Affairs.* 2 vols. American State Papers. Documents, Legislative and

Executive, of the Congress of the United States; Class II. Washington, D.C.: Gales and Seaton. [Volume 1: 1st Cong. – 13th Cong., 25 May 1789 to 25 Oct 1814; comps. and eds. Walter Lowrie and Matthew St. Clair Clarke. Volume 2: 14th Cong. – 19th Cong., 6 Dec. 1815 to 1 Mar. 1827; comps. and eds. Walter Lowrie and Walter S. Franklin.]

[252] United States, Indian Claims Commission. 1974. "Commission Findings [on the Chippewa Indians]." In *Chippewa Indians VII,* comp. and ed. David Agee Horr, pp. 9–548. [Findings of fact and opinion.] See [98].

[253] United States National Archives and Records Service. 1972. *The American Indian; Select Catalogue of National Archives Microfilm Publications.* National Archives Publication No. 72-27. Washington, D.C.: National Archives and Records Service, General Service Administration.

Verwyst, Chrysostom (Christian Adrian).

[254] 1886. *Missionary Labors of Fathers Marquette, Menard, and Allouez in the Lake Superior Region.* Milwaukee, and Chicago: Hoffman Bros.

[255] 1900. *Life and Labors of the Rt. Rev. Frederick Baraga, First Bishop of Marquette, Mich.; To Which Are Added Short Sketches of the Lives and Labors of*

Other Indian Missionaries of the Northwest . . . Milwaukee: M. H. Wiltzius and Co.

[256] 1916. "A Glossary of Chippewa Indian Names of Rivers, Lakes, and Villages." *Acta et Dicta* 4:253–74.

*[257] Vizenor, Gerald Robert. 1972. *The Everlasting Sky; New Voices from the People Named the Chippewa.* New York: Crowell–Collier Press.

Vizenor, Gerald Robert, ed.

*[258] 1965. *Anishenabe Adisokan; Tales of the People.* Minneapolis: Nodin Press.

*[259] 1965. *Anishenabe Nagomen; Songs of the People.* Minneapolis: Nodin Press.

*[260] Walker, Louise Jean. 1959. *Legends of Green Sky Hill.* Illustrated by Grace Hoyt. Grand Rapids, Mich.: Eerdmans.

[261] Warner, Robert M. and Groesbeck, Lois J. 1974. "Historical Report on the Sault Ste. Marie Area." In *Chippewa Indians V,* comp. and ed. David Agee Horr, pp. 319–77. See [98].

Warren, William Whipple.

[262] 1854. "Oral Traditions Respecting the History of the Ojibwa Nation." In *Historical and Statistical Information Respecting the History, Conditions and Prospects of the Indian Tribes of the United States,* ed. Henry Rowe Schoolcraft, vol. 2, pp. 135–67. See [239].

[263] 1885. "History of the Ojibways Based upon Traditions and Oral Statements." *Collections of the Minnesota Historical Society* 5:21–394.

[264] Webber, William L. 1896. "Indian Cession of 1819, Made by the Treaty of Saginaw." *Collections and Researches made by the Michigan Pioneer and Historical Society* 26:517–34. [The Webber article was presented at the 1895 meeting of the Society.]

[265] Wheeler-Voegelin, Erminie. 1974. "An Ethnohistorical Report on the Indian Use and Occupancy of *Royce Area 53* . . . and of *Royce Area 54* . . ." In *Indians of Northern Ohio and Southeastern Michigan,* comp. and ed. David Agee Horr, pp. 51–316. See [98].

[266] Wheeler-Voegelin, Erminie and Hickerson, Harold. 1974. "The Red Lake and Pembina Chippewa." In *Chippewa Indians I,* comp. and ed. David Agee Horr, pp. 25–230. See [98].

[267] Whipple, Henry Benjamin. 1901. "Civilization and Christianization of the Ojibways in Minnesota." *Collections of the Minnesota Historical Society* 9:129–42.

[268] Whittlesey, Charles. 1884/85. "Among the Otchipwees." *Magazine of Western History* 1:86–91; 177–92; and 335–42.

*[269] Wilcox, Arthur T. 1953. "The Chippewa Sugar Camp." *Michigan History* 37:276–85.

[270] Wilson, Edward F. 1886. *Missionary Work Among the Ojebway Indians . . .* London: The Society for Promoting Christian Knowledge; and New York: E. and J. B. Young and Co.

[271] Winchell, Newton Horace. 1911. *The Aborigines of Minnesota; A Report Based on the Collections of Jacob V. Brower, and on the Field Surveys and Notes of Alfred J. Hill and Theodore H. Lewis . . .* St. Paul, Minn.: The Minnesota Historical Society [The Pioneer Co. Print.].

[272] Wold, Pauline. 1943. "Some Recollections of the Leech Lake Uprising." *Minnesota History* 24: 142–48.

[273] Wood, Edwin Orin. 1916. *History of Genessee County, Michigan; Her People, Industries and Institutions . . . With Biographical Sketches of Representative Citizens and Genealogical Records of Many of the Old Families . . .* 2 vols. Indianapolis: Federal Pub. Co.

[274] Woolworth, Nancy Louise. 1965. "The Grand Portage Mission: 1731–1965." *Minnesota History* 39:301–10.

[275] Wright, J. V. 1965. "A Regional Examination of Ojibwa Culture History." *Anthropologica* 7: 189–227.

The Newberry Library
Center for the History of the American Indian

Director: Francis Jennings

Established in 1972 by the Newberry Library, in conjunction with the Committee on Institutional Cooperation of eleven midwestern universities, the Center makes the resources of one of America's foremost research libraries in the Humanities available to those interested in improving the quality and effectiveness of teaching American Indian history. The Newberry's collections include some 100,000 volumes on the history of the American Indian and offer specialized resources for studying historical aspects of Indian–White relations and Indian linguistics. The Center also assists Native Americans engaged in writing tribal histories and developing educational materials.